Praise for **Pitching**

"A route map of the obstacle[s]
practised navigator. This boo[k]
that is commonly left behind in the whirlwind.

Oliver Bolitho, Managing Director, UK Institutional Business,
Goldman Sachs Asset Management International

"This book will be invaluable for anyone in professional services
looking to improve their win rate. Applying these principles
in a disciplined way will help the novice and experienced
professional alike."

William Stancer, Global Director of Marketing Resources, Accenture

"Want to win that new client? Clinch that deal? Here's a
plain-talking guide to the art of business pitching which
should be compulsory reading for the whole team."

Neil Harnby, Partner, Linklaters

"*Pitching to Win* is the quintessential book on pitching and
winning new business, written by one of the world's authoritative
practitioners. It is required reading for anyone making new
business presentations – a definitive guide on how to do it right."

Tom Watson, former Vice Chairman of Omnicom

"If I was a client, I'd make sure any agency pitching to me had
read this book."

Dominic Mills, Editorial Director of Campaign,
Marketing and Media Week

"Winning new business is the single most defining attribute of the
truly iconic companies in any category. Lots of people have tried to
distill and bottle those elements that make the essential difference
between success and nowhere. David Kean has written the only
book I have ever read that gets close to giving me real insights into
a critical part of the process of winning. I wish this book had been
written decades ago."

Peter Mead, co-founder, Abbott Mead Vickers BBDO

"I wish I'd written it."   **Martin Jones, AAR**

PITCHING TO WIN

The art of winning new business

DAVID KEAN

Marshall Cavendish
Business

Copyright © 2008 David Kean

Reprinted 2010

First published by Marshall Cavendish/Cyan as How Not to Come Second.

This edition published by Marshall Cavendish Business
An imprint of Marshall Cavendish International

PO Box 65829
London EC1P 1NY
United Kingdom
info@marshallcavendish.co.uk

and

1 New Industrial Road
Singapore 536196
genrefsales@sg.marshallcavendish.com
www.marshallcavendish.com/genref

Marshall Cavendish is a trademark of Times Publishing Limited

Other Marshall Cavendish offices:
Marshall Cavendish International (Asia) Private Limited, 1 New Industrial Road,
Singapore 536196 • Marshall Cavendish Corporation. 99 White Plains Road,
Tarrytown NY 10591-9001, USA • Marshall Cavendish International (Thailand) Co
Ltd. 253 Asoke, 12th Floor, Sukhumvit 21 Road, Klongtoey Nua, Wattana, Bangkok
10110, Thailand • Marshall Cavendish (Malaysia) Sdn Bhd, Times Subang, Lot 46,
Subang Hi-Tech Industrial Park, Batu Tiga, 40000 Shah Alam, Selangor Darul Ehsan,
Malaysia

A CIP record for this book is available from the British Library

ISBN 978-1-905736-24-9

Printed and bound in Great Britain by
CPI Bookmarque, Croydon CR0 4TD

Acknowledgments

I have been immensely privileged in my career to have what all salesmen pray for: brilliant products to sell. Having a great product to sell does give you a distinct advantage in winning pitches. So, to all those hugely talented souls, the thinkers, the creatives, the account handlers, the public relations professionals, the digirati, the direct mail specialists, the advertising gurus, the boys and girls in "meedya," the branding folk—thank you. We work in a fabulous industry—the communications industry—full of fascinating, talented, civilized people, which has much to offer the business world. Thank you for making my work life both stimulating and easy.

Special thanks are due to a coterie of friends and colleagues who have been so generous with their time in suggesting improvements and pointing out the numerous gaping holes in my knowledge and logic: Neil and Lorna for their honesty and enthusiasm, William for his immensely practical additions, Dominic for injecting some fun, Martin for the details that make all the difference, Saad and Cameron for their cultural radar, Brian and Sian for their governmental expertise, Tom for his wise counsel, and for making me start all over again. To Andy for the introduction to a publisher that would publish me, Janice for helping me move from quill and ink into the 21st century, Liz and Rachel for their editing skills, and, most of all, to Messrs Cowpe and Stratton, for your friendship, encouragement, and tutelage.

This book is dedicated to my two Inspector Morses, from your ever-grateful Sergeant Lewis.

Contents

Preface:
What's this book about?

I work in the most exciting business in the world: the persuasion business. You work in it too. Everybody does. Every day.

Persuading people of our point of view and getting them to back our judgment with their money is what makes the business world go round—whether you're a budding entrepreneur with a startup idea, a writer selling a script, a lawyer with a point of view, or a multinational marketeer pushing your flavor of beans over the competitor's. And the sharpest end of the persuasion business is the pitch. That intense and brief period when you get to make your case. How you make the most of that opportunity is what this book is about.

Pitch

Definition from Oxford English Dictionary:
(noun) a form of words used when trying to persuade someone to buy or accept something
(verb) make a bid to obtain a contract or other business

Real meaning:
beauty parade

PART 1
Getting it wrong

Chapter 1
A very close second

The call, when it comes, isn't a surprise. "Hi. I'm calling about the pitch you made to us last week. I'd like to say how much we enjoyed your presentation; we thought your ideas were really interesting. And we thought your people were great too." By now you know what's coming. The next word the prospective client utters is going to be "But."

"But … this time, I'm afraid you came a very close second."

Four weeks of your life, hundreds of man hours, tens of thousands of euros of billable time. Angst, heartache, slog. Disrupted work life. Disrupted home life. The cost and consequence of three little words. **Very. Close. Second.**

Let's be honest: nearly winning is called losing.

These unpalatable words are heard far too often in business. And what makes them even more unpalatable is that they aren't even true. You didn't come a close second. You lost. The prospective client is just being nice. It's human nature—he doesn't want to make you feel even worse than he knows you feel right now. So he's kind. He says you nearly won. **Let's be honest: nearly winning is called losing.** Do not take succor from the client's kindness. Do not scuttle back to your team and tell them you came a close second. If you delude yourself, your team, and your company into feeling OK about coming a close second, you'll *always* lose. This sort of delusion is what psychiatrists call "being in denial." And no one can heal while they deny there's a problem in the first place. Stop living in denial! Think about what winning the pitch equivalent of the silver medal really means. The American comedian Jerry Seinfeld sums it up best:

I think I have a problem with that silver medal. I think if I was an Olympic athlete I would rather come in last than win the silver . . . You know, you win the gold, you feel good. You win the bronze, at least you think "I got something." But you win that silver, that's like: "Congratulations, you almost won! Of all the losers, you came first in that group. You're the number 1 loser. No one lost ahead of you." And they always have that photo finish. And there's always silver . . . gold. Greatest guy in the world . . . **never heard of him.**

Source: Jerry Seinfeld, *I'm Telling You for the Last Time*, 1998, Universal Records Inc.

Losing hurts. All that effort; all those man hours; all that expense. When you add it all up, it's like driving a brand new BMW—with all the extras—off the roof of your office building.

And do you know the strangest thing of all? **It takes less effort to win than to come a close second.** Less effort, but more focus. Don't believe me? Think about it. If you keep on doing your pitches in the same old way, getting the same dire results, how hard and debilitating is that? How much simpler to copy the proven techniques that deliver victory. Don't reinvent the wheel every time. Be lazy. Do what works.

This book will help you win more, more of the time. Implement the ideas you read about in this book and you, your colleagues, and your company won't drive so many BMWs off the roof and into the pavement below.

The Moviestore Collection

Who cares? I care.

Why do I care? I've seen the transformation of individuals and businesses as they get out of old, ineffective habits to enjoy vastly improved results by adopting the approach taught in this book.

I care because I like to see people get a better result. I care because getting better results boosts people's confidence and self-esteem, and knits individuals into teams. I care because I hate to see brilliance and effort go to waste. Great ideas that can make a difference take too much sweat to hazard on a throw of the dice. Great ideas deserve a chance to shine. I care about winning pitches because only when its creator has won a pitch can a great idea become reality. And I get really annoyed with the mediocrity of most companies' pitches and their lackluster attitude to pitching.

Pitching really matters.

Chapter 2
Why bother?

Rumors of the death of the pitch have been around a long time. Everybody moans that pitching is expensive and wasteful. Fact is, the pitch is here to stay. You may think it unfair, you may not like it, but it is the best system business has for deciding between competing ideas and the suppliers of those ideas. Like democracy, it may not be perfect but it works most of the time and it is preferable to any other system in use. So what's the benefit?

If you invest the effort to be brilliant at pitching, you get a host of miracle spin-offs. You win lots of business. In turn, this attracts attention to you and your company. More clients want to see what's so special about you. You win more new business. You become "hot." Your success becomes a talent magnet. Your existing clients get a reassuring, warm feeling that they are working with a winner. They give you more work. Your teams feel confident. They produce better work for their clients. You get higher, more profitable fees. You start to dent the confidence of your competitors. It's a gloriously virtuous circle.

When you get in the habit of winning pitches you tilt the playing field massively in your favor. You are like the Brazilian soccer team. When you walk on the pitch your opposition feels one nil down before the start whistle has even blown.

Winning pitches turbo-charges your success like nothing else.

Chapter 3
Winning pitches is easy: be lazy

Winning pitches is easy. It is certainly no more work than losing them. We just need to put the effort in the right places.

On the average winter's day, you will don 11 items of clothing. If, every day, you were to put them on in a different—still sensible—order, you'd have thousands of variations to choose from. (If you put them on in any order, there'd be millions of possible variations.)

Luckily, your brain short circuits this process. You dress the way you always dress: on autopilot and in the same dress order as every other day. We are creatures of habit.

Unfortunately, this tends to mean we pitch the same way as we dress, on autopilot, using the same formula as last time (whether it worked or not). And we are surprised when we get the phone call saying "Great presentation, interesting ideas but … this time you came a very close second." Habit is good. Just make sure it is the right habit.

What follows are the habits of some of the world's great pitchers. These are the habits that produce better success rates for their practitioners. These are the habits to get into, the habits that work. Be lazy, copy them.

But before you cure yourself of bad habits, you have to know what you're doing wrong. Once you know what's wrong, you can correct your behavior and get results.

WINNING

Chapter 4
What's it all about, Alfie?

What is pitching all about? Whenever I ask this question there is an avalanche of answers.

> To show our skills.
> To give the client the answer.
> To demonstrate our talent.
> To crack the problem.
> To produce amazing work.
> To get the client to like us.
> To grow our business.
> To grow ourselves.
> To learn.
> To practice being a team.

Pitching isn't about any of these things. These are just means to the real end, or nice side effects of pitching. When it comes down to it, pitching is really only about one thing.

That's it. Everything else is academic if you don't win. Failing to understand this simple truth and—more importantly—failing to act on it, is the first mistake all losing teams make.

Why is it important to know and remember that pitching is only about winning?

Because it makes you focus on the result. Because **focusing on the result means you adopt the behaviors and attitudes that make the winning result much more likely. This is "total" pitching. It requires total commitment to the result; it is not an amateur endeavor. It is not a hobby.** Being entirely focused on winning means you *have* to behave in a certain way. There are no "might dos" or "probably shoulds" about someone committed to winning. They do what they know must be done in order to win. Being dedicated to winning means living your life in a particular way. Ask any professional sportsperson. An athlete aiming for an Olympic gold medal doesn't get up and think "Maybe I'll go on a training run today. I'll see how I feel. I'll see if I can squeeze it in." As Yoda said:

> Do, or do not. There is no "try."

Victory belongs to those who understand this simple truth. Until you win, nothing else can happen; nothing else matters. And to win, you have to do all the hard work, which means you *deserve* to win.

If you are not 100% committed to winning, then don't pitch.

Chapter 5
Hands up, all the amateurs

Time was when there were Gentlemen and Players. Amateurs and Professionals. The done thing was to be a Gentleman. Players were regarded as vulgar. Players practiced. They trained. They took it seriously. They expended effort to improve and hone their skills.

How much better, went the thinking, how much more civilized, **to triumph effortlessly**.

Times have changed. No one in sport nowadays would subscribe to this view. And in business it's the same. We all take pride in being professionals now. If I asked a room full of businesspeople to raise their hands if they thought themselves to be amateurs at doing their job, do you think many hands would go up? Hopefully not.

And yet, when it comes to pitching, we behave like amateurs. We've allowed ourselves to slip into bad habits.

We have a pitch in two weeks. We stall reading the brief and do something more urgent instead. Two days go by before we get around to reading it and getting the pitch team together to discuss it. We only had ten working days to start with; now we've got eight left. We've wasted 20% of the time available. (If your competitors got together the moment the brief came in, they're two days ahead of you. Oops.)

As a team, we meet when we can. The whole team can never meet at the same time in the same room until the actual pitch day—they're all too busy (being "busy fools").

Of the eight days available, we spend 80% worrying away at the client problem and coming up with a solution. That leaves us a day and a half to research our idea, write the presentation, rehearse it (which happens only once, if at all, in the wee small hours, the day of the pitch), write the document, and produce any other materials we might need to bring the presentation to life.

We agree who is going to say what, and make last-minute amendments to the presentation, on our journey to the client's offices.

And we call ourselves professionals.

This is how 90% of pitches are done, and why 90% of phone calls end with "I'm afraid that this time you came a very close second."

Doing everything at the last minute is our disease. It is the mark of the amateur. If you want to stop driving BMW cars off your office roof, **start acting like a professional**.

> **Don't do it all at the last minute.**

Chapter 6
Olympic gold

What's the difference between a 100-meter Olympic gold medalist and the silver medalist?

Do you think the silver medalist was delighted that, after 16 years of training, after losing most of his childhood and all of his adulthood to training five times a day, after 5,844 days—that's 93,504 waking hours and 46,752 hours asleep—dreaming about winning gold, he came a close second?

Me neither.

A close second is a million miles off. First is first. Second is nowhere.

Pitching is like the final of the 100-meter sprint. In a pitch, just as in the sprint, you have to get through the qualifying rounds to win a place in the final contest. In a pitch, just as in the sprint, you have a finite period (or distance) in which to win. In a pitch, just as in the sprint, you need to get off the blocks faster and cleaner than all your competitors. In a 100-meter race, if you come off the blocks slowly you'll never make up the lost ground—you'll have lost almost before you begin. In a pitch, if you don't get around to reading the client's brief until day 2 of your allotted ten days, that's like giving your world-class competitors a 10-meter head start in the 100-meter race. Why would you do that? And yet time after time after time that's exactly what we do. We let other more urgent stuff get in the way. Meantime, our competitors are steaming off down the track leaving us behind. It's crazy behavior. And most pitchers end up being surprised when they get the call telling them they came a "very close second."

Preparation on the day

Do you think that athletes travel straight from the Olympic Village, de-bus, strip out of their tracksuits, get down on the starter blocks, and—**POW!**—explode up the lane to the finish line in record time?

No. They don't. They warm up. They psyche themselves into the "zone"—that mental space where they know they will win. They loosen their limbs and stretch their

Getty Images

muscles. They focus. They close their eyes and run the race for the millionth time in their heads. They block out the crowds. Or use them to pump up the adrenalin.

You can do the same when you pitch. Shake your limbs out. Go to a quiet corner of the office and jog on the spot. Think that's weird? All you're doing is getting your body ready to perform. And one of the most important muscles you'll be relying on is your tongue. Stretch it! Give it a tongue twister to grapple with, then you won't get to your feet and emit a high-pitched squeak, or kick off with "Er …" or "Um …" *Er* and *um* are the presentational equivalent of an athlete tripping as he comes off the blocks. It's a bad way to start a race and a sad way to start a pitch.

Chapter 7
What do clients want from us?

Add up all the de-briefs from clients, all the experience of pitchers, and all the wisdom of the consultants and intermediaries who sit at the client's right hand through the painful pitch process, and what does it all boil down to?

Clients are no different from you and me. If you're looking for a business partner, what do you want?

> You want a **team** of people who get on well and who spark off each other.

> You want people who have made the effort to understand **you** and **your business**.

> You want to work with people who will make it **interesting, stimulating, and fun**.

> You want people who **share your ambition** for your goal.

> You want **value** for money.

> You want people who get the answers right and **solve your problems** creatively.

Six components. But usually, only one of these gets any attention from pitching companies. Guess which one.

Solving the problem

Solving the problem gets 70% to 85% of the time available. Why? Because it's the interesting bit. It's the bit you are paid to do. The bit the clients can't do themselves.

If you focus entirely on solving the problem, I've got a nasty surprise for you.

Solving the problem doesn't win pitches.

All the other stuff wins pitches. Behaving like a **team**. **Understanding *them*** as people. (Get to know their agendas, the politics at play in the organization; get to know them as individuals, their prejudices and concerns, their hopes, fears, and beliefs.) Being **enjoyable** to work alongside: not precious, but stimulating, collaborative, and energetic. Clients want to buy people they can get on with—personable and friendly people who would be interesting company on a long-haul flight.

Sharing the client's **ambition** for their organization. Clients, just like us, love people who make the extra effort to help. Who get into the trenches with them rather than looking down from the lofty heights of their ivory tower. An example of how to do this comes from a story about the flamboyant CEO of a London advertising agency that worked for a major cellphone network. A few weeks before Christmas, which is the key selling period for this client, the CEO arranged to go work behind the counter of one of the client's busiest shops. He spent half a day selling phones and subscriptions (this is the CEO, remember). When he went back to his desk in the afternoon, he sent an email to his client, the chairman of this vast organization. In the email he explained what he had done, itemized the top ten most frequently asked questions and the top three most common complaints, and then offered five or six recommendations on how this organization could sell more subscriptions, based on his experience that morning. Who would you rather have working on your business if you were a client? This guy, or a CEO who you know has never visited your shop? Easy choice.

These are the areas the pitching professional focuses on. **This is where the money is.** Sure, you've got to be able to answer the exam question. But that's the price of entry. That's why you set up in business. That's what you promise just by being there. It is not enough. The soft stuff around the edges is where you win the gold medal.

Why do we keep losing to inferior competitors?

Have you ever wondered why your company loses to inferior competition? Again and again, I see companies that are phenomenally good practitioners of their craft discipline, that produce demonstrably superior results for their clients and have cleverer people than their competitors, but they still lose pitch after pitch to companies only half as good as they are. Why?

Because the competitors **compensate for their skill gap with stunningly good pitch craft**. They know they are unlikely to produce a better solution than you. So they focus on all the softer stuff that you are ignoring:

getting to understand the client and what makes them tick; fizzing with energy and effort to show the client what a dynamic team he will get; having a laugh—with the client rather than with their own team. These competitors will spend their time being the **embodiment of great value**.

When I ask companies to list what they are good at in a pitch and then list what their (inferior) competitors are better at, I always get the same list. Companies that are technically brilliant problem solvers focus on the technicalities and solving the problem. (Big surprise.) Their competitors, who aren't as technically proficient, **focus on putting on a fantastic show**. It's like the difference between high-street fashion retailers. Some fashion retailers have dazzling window displays—sexy, funky, ever-changing, and exciting. But the merchandise is often shoddily made and doesn't last. Other retailers I could mention have the dullest, dreariest shop window displays but their merchandise is well made, robust, and excellent value. The trouble is, customers like the excitement of the sexy window display. So they choose inferior goods because the **promise** of the experience is superior. Think how powerful you'd be if you had **great merchandise *and* a sexy window display**. If you could put a sheen of showmanship on your palpably superior product, you'd win every pitch.

Dazzle the client. Learn from your inferior competitors: dazzle the client by doing the "soft" stuff superbly.

Chapter 8
Seven ready-made excuses for coming a close second

If you're doing amateur pitches at the last minute, and you're not dazzling the client, it's inevitable you'll get lots of "close second" telephone calls.

When the inevitable happens, when the call comes and you have to trudge down the corridor to console your team, who have been waiting with bated breath for the result, when that happens, here are some easy options to help them feel better about the news.

1 The clients weren't ready for our solution.

2 They "bought" a particular individual at our competitor.

3 We are too big for them.

4 We are too small for them.

5 It was a stitch-up. We never had a chance.

6 They think we are too expensive.

7 The client is an idiot.

1 The clients weren't ready for our solution

They thought we were too brave, too radical, too revolutionary for their organization. This just means you didn't find out what they wanted, or felt they needed, and the other guys did. You didn't match your solution to their **perceived** need.

2 They "bought" a particular individual at our competitor

Someone at the opposition knocked their socks off. Someone at your competitor actually communicated with them and got through. He didn't just **present at them** like you did. He made contact, spoke to them like human beings and **communicated with them**. (There is a massive difference between presenting and communicating.)

3 We are too big for them

They want a boutique and to work with the founding bosses of the company. (You didn't wow them and the opposition did.)

4 We are too small for them

They want a one-size-fits-all international network, not a boutique. (You didn't wow them and the opposition did.)

Think: why were you on the pitch list if you didn't fit their selection criteria?

5 It was a stitch-up. We never had a chance

(A: We were the incumbent.) They just asked us to re-pitch out of misguided courtesy. They were always going to give it to their new favorite.

(B: They gave it back to the incumbent.) They never intended to give the business out to a new partner; they just used us for free ideas and to get the incumbent to sharpen their prices.

By the way, **you can win it back if you are the incumbent**. Just under a sixth of incumbents keep the client. (Source: Advertising Agency Register: AAR.) The rule of pitching as the incumbent is "**don't look back in anger**." It is tempting to resent the client for making you re-pitch after all that wonderful work you've done for them, and after they gave you five out of five in the client satisfaction survey you conducted last month. But you'll show that resentment by reminding the client of what you've done for them. Be gracious: **they feel uncomfortable too**. Don't dwell on the past in your pitch. **Pitches are about the future.** And **change the team**: new people see new opportunities—they're not blinded to new ideas by overfamiliarity with the minutiae. They will also fizz with enthusiasm, which the old team won't do.

6 They think we are too expensive

The other guys dropped their pants. We can't compete on price.

Maybe the competitors did sharpen their pencils more than you. Maybe. But you can always resolve money issues. They are never the sole criterion for purchase, not in pitches for professional services. If you pitched and the client isn't interested in talking money and terms very soon after, it's a bad sign. They haven't fallen in love with you. (The subject of pricing is covered in more detail in chapter 13.)

7 The client is an idiot

It's so tempting to have a moaning session about the client. How they couldn't spot a strategy if it hit them between the eyes. How they didn't grasp the import of what you were saying. How they failed to see your brilliance.

Were they an idiot when they invited you to pitch? No. They were wise, intelligent, incisive clients back then! What changed? Who's the idiot: you or them? You had the chance and you blew it. Let's stop being in denial.

> These are excuses, and they are all preventable. Let's focus on how to prevent them ever being made in your company again.

PART 2

Getting it right

Chapter 9
Ingredients for successful pitching

There are only eight ingredients of a successful pitch. Do them all well and you will win a lot more business.

1 Be organized
2 Know your audience
3 Solve the problem
4 Price properly
5 Practice
6 Great presentations
7 Unstoppable momentum
8 Feedback

Each one of these will be dealt with in the following chapters. The trick is to get into the **habit** of **doing them all** so your company believes *this is the way we run new business pitches around here*.

If you don't institutionalize these eight habits, you will very quickly disappear down **the path to hell** which, as we all know, is paved with good intentions. It is that strange paradox of human nature—we know what works, and we mean to do it, but somehow we just don't get around to it.

As the saying goes: **Just do it.**

Chapter 10
Be organized

Time. It has a habit of running out. **Use time**, don't squander it. Being organized makes the most of the time available.

When is the ideal time to start work on the client's brief for a pitch?

You have very limited time. (Remember, it's like the 100-meter sprint.) You must use that time to advantage. Yes, you've got urgent emails from clients; colleagues are demanding your attention; you're needed in ten places at once; you're project managing a huge job for a very important existing client. These are all reasonable excuses.

But the whole pitch process is **unreasonable**. It is carried out at breakneck speed as a **"speed dating"** exercise. It is fast, frenetic, frightening, false, and unforgiving. It is not for the fainthearted. But it is also exciting, adrenalin-pumping, and physically and intellectually demanding. It is not open to reason. You are either up for it or out of it.

Remember, if you are to have any chance of winning you must **MAKE THE AVAILABLE TIME WORK FOR YOU**. (At the end of this book are week-by-week timetables to help you stay on target.)

Here is what you need to do:

1 Organize diaries

Pretty prosaic stuff, huh? Everyone rushes to do the brilliant bit and no one thinks about the basics. Successful generals know that organization and planning on the battlefront are the key to victory. If you don't believe me, remember The Charge of the Light Brigade.

If you have two weeks, you need to **meet every day**. Come in early, go home late—but meet. Get those meetings in your team's diaries immediately. And make sure you schedule three (yes three) full rehearsal sessions. Why three? I'll explain this in chapter 14: *Practice*.

Get the pitch date and time in the team's diaries. **And, during the period of the pitch, get at least one formal meeting a week into the client's diaries.** You can always explain that you will cancel if you don't need it, but get it in their schedules. (You will need it and you must have it.) It is your chance to gel with them, to test their reactions, opinions, attitudes, and strategies, and to pre-sell your approach to their problem. **(If they won't let you meet them, don't pitch. You are wasting your time.)** If they're being difficult about meeting, you must find a way because your opposition will find a way. (Remember, your opposition *have* to get close to the client because they're not going to solve the problem as well as you will.)

Explain to the person who is blocking access that:

a) you only pitch if you get access

b) getting access to the senior clients will mean that your solution will be much better (How can you solve their problem if they won't talk to you?)

c) this person will look good for fielding top-level companies that give his bosses a choice between excellent solutions.

> **They can hide but we will find them!**

Time and again I've seen companies pull out of pitches when they've been told they cannot meet the clients, only to get a call from the client saying that they can have the meeting and would they please pitch! Stop worrying whether the client will think you are being pushy. You're going to lose anyway if you don't meet the client, so go for it. A colleague from Lisbon exhibited exactly the right approach when he said **"They can hide but we will find them!"**

2 Get your pitch bible out to the team

This is a compendium of all the relevant material each member of the pitch team must know to get them up to speed on the project as fast as possible. It should include:

> The client brief

> Desk research on the market, the organization, and the competition

> Press clippings on the client organization and any articles where individuals from the organization are quoted

> Biographies of the people who will be on the pitch panel, any relationships you have with them and what you know about them

> Examples of the work the client has been producing with their existing partners

> Summaries of any conversations you have had with the client about the brief

> An analysis of your competitors, and why the client might have asked them to pitch

> A detailed timing plan for your pitch with all the key dates and deadlines

> List of issues to be resolved, questions to be asked, actions to be taken, people to be met

and **PECSTEL**—an analysis of the issues facing the organization:

Political (internal and external)

Economic (macro/micro economic issues affecting the client's business)

Consumer & Competitive (trends and activity)

Socio-demographic (social and population trends affecting performance in the future)

Technology (impact on market sector and players)

Environmental (threats and opportunities)

Legislative (threats and opportunities)

This can all be distilled into a **SWOT** (Strengths, Weaknesses, Opportunities, Threats) analysis of the organization so that you have a clear view of the key issues.

3 Get your team together

Don't wait for the client to fire the starter pistol before
starting. If you can steal a time advantage by getting
going before the client's brief arrives, then get going.
But whatever you do, line up your team and get them
together *immediately* to get everyone up on the issues
and the plan of attack, and to brainstorm an approach
to winning. Make time your ally, not your enemy.

4 Get your team right

Often, the team is composed of whoever is available. If
so, you might as well not pitch. To start with, you need to
make sure that the **chemistry** between members of your
own team is excellent. Do these people get on? Do they
have complementary skills and personalities? Have they
worked well together previously?

Then think about the personalities of the client team and
try to get your team to **complement and balance that
structure**. So many times we field inappropriate mixes of
people who are not compatible with the clients. Is the
client's organization young at heart, or formal? Lean and
fit, or slow and deliberate? Cerebral, or action oriented?
Male or female biased? Progressive or traditional? High-
tech or old school? Do they use a sales vocabulary, or a
brand vocabulary, or a creative vocabulary, or do they talk
purely in financial terms? Are they a big organization
interested in evolution, or a young upstart interested in
revolution? Do they have a range of personalities? For
example, if you are pitching to act on behalf of a
company pension fund, you will be pitching to people

with widely differing levels of technical knowledge and utterly different perspectives. The financial director and the union representative may have hugely differing expectations, and may need to be communicated with in different ways. Your team needs to relate to both types.

Make an analysis of the organization and its pitch panel to gauge the right mix for your team.

Every member of your team must have a specific and defined role in the pitch. You may need some gray-hairs to demonstrate gravitas and experience. You may need youth to represent the client's target audience. You will need a numerate business head. You might need a firebrand to signal drive. What's the right balance between male and female? Whatever, casting is key.

One company lost a government pitch focused on nursing because the company's CEO, a woman, turned up flanked by nine male "suits." What does this tell you about their attitude and approach to the task? Their likely empathy with the target audience: nurses?

Think about it.

5 Make pitching a badge of honor

This process will be helped if senior management impresses upon the pitch team the honor that has been bestowed upon them in being asked to work on this very important pitch. Working on a pitch should be seen as a milestone in your career. Each member of the team should also be told that, in order to win, the company's resources are at their disposal and that they have the full support of management.

You can only promise blood, toil, sweat, and tears. But the tears will be sweeter if the blood, toil, and sweat lead to victory. Clear the decks, and **put someone in charge who will make the pitch everyone else's number one priority**. There is nothing like a **charming thug** to force through the action necessary to yield victory. Every company should have one.

6 Meet regularly, religiously

Schedule a daily team meeting. When you meet together, please get someone to take notes of what is agreed. So much time (that you haven't got) is wasted remembering what was said at the last meeting and who was supposed to do what by when. If you keep notes, you'll build momentum consistently rather than in fits and starts. It has always amused me that for the *really* big and sexy pitches, companies will find the time to do this. But if you are not finding the time to do this on all the pitches you are making, why are you pitching? You're likely to lose the pitch anyway—and that really is time you can't afford.

Get together as a team. Every day.

7 Brainstorm the brief with your top talent

Within 24 hours of receiving the client's brief, and having circulated it internally to the members of the team, get together with your company's most senior people and brainstorm the possible solutions.

You won't get it right. But you will get it right enough to **crack 70% of the solution**. Experienced colleagues have seen most problems before, in one form or another. They can save you time because they can prevent you reinventing the wheel. You will emerge from this brainstorm with a set of hypotheses and some unanswered questions, but with enough to have broken the back of the issue.

So many losing pitch teams either worry away at the problem for far too long or leave the thinking until far too late.

Starting early allows the right side of your brain (the "creative/imaginative" part) to cogitate for longer, and creative solutions do take time to develop. The left side of your brain, the organizing side, can order thoughts very quickly. It needs less time. So start now and you maximize the chance of getting an original and compelling solution.

8 Network like crazy

Use your contacts to do some detective work. Someone, somewhere will know the client. Find out the politics in the organization. Why is there a pitch? What is the client's board worrying about? Find out the real issues behind the brief.

9 Find your mole

You need a mole at the client. Often the most neglected
and overlooked person on the client team is the personal
assistant. Make friends with that person. He might come
in very handy after the pitch.

10 Look after the intermediary

It is estimated that 25% to 40% of all client companies,
and 60% of big client companies, use intermediaries
when searching for a new advertising agency. (Source:
Haymarket Publishing Services Ltd.) The Royal Institute
of British Architects (RIBA) receives over 1,400
commercial inquiries every year from potential clients
looking for architects. RIBA helps these potential clients
draw up a shortlist of architectural practices that may be
appropriate to the client's needs. The Institute is an
important constituency to keep on side because it is a
potential source of business and an objective adviser to
the client community.

So if you're a firm of architects in Britain, and you want
to be in the consideration list, you'll need to ensure RIBA
is kept up to date on your capabilities and on your
suitability for particular types of brief. In short, you'll
need to look after the relationship you have with the
professional or trade organization, whichever profession
you work in. These people are very, very important.
Ensure you know them, cherish their goodwill, inform
them about what you are doing, and grill them for their
perspective on the client.

Chapter 11
Know your audience

The key to winning a pitch is to win the hearts and minds of the *real* target audience.

> **The real target audience of the pitch is the CLIENT.**

Pitch after pitch, we see the same fundamental mistake being made. **Pitching companies think the target audience is the audience that the client is trying to influence**—the housewife, the shareholder, the investor, the employee, the small businessperson, journalists, politicians. Whoever. In a logical world, this would be quite proper and correct.

Logic has nothing to do with pitching.

Successful pitching companies know that they are really trying to **win the votes of the clients on the judging panel**. These people are the audience to influence. **Ninety percent of the ideas presented in pitches never come to fruition.** (Source: AAR.) They are ideas that capture the hearts and minds of the client, but are superseded by ideas that are more appropriate to the actual task *after* the business is won.

This is a subtle business. This is where the true pitching professional comes into his own. **If organization and logistics is the science of pitching, understanding the client is the art of pitching.**

Let's talk about the client.

Clients are egocentric, opinionated, and in love with the sound of their own voice. They are full of prejudice—they have views on virtually every facet of what you will present. They like people like them; they like to be involved; they react well to people who make an effort. They want value.

In short, they are just like you and me. Whether they wear a pinstripe Savile Row suit or a baggy jumper and sandals, they are human beings. And human beings have been motivated by the same fundamental things for tens of thousands of years. Remember the list of what clients are looking for (page 19)? It is no coincidence that they want a team of people who understand them and their issues and who will be stimulating to work with. They want people who get on well with each other, and spark off each other. **In other words, they want like-minded people to help them pursue a common goal.**

Why you must get to know the client

You have only a few days. Victory will go to the side that gets to know the client best. The side that identifies the real decision maker on the client team (the one who has the most votes on the panel) and finds out what he wants. The side that identifies the language and style the client employs. The culture of the company. The politics in the boardroom. The side that builds confidence and trust, and determines the client's likes and dislikes; that involves the client in the solution. They will win.

Why is all this so important?

Because each client is subtly different. By spending time
with them, by getting under their skin, the pitch team
can **feel** their way to what the client wants and needs.
You are like the doctor, asking questions, asking more
questions, testing here, probing there, in order to zero in
on the right diagnosis.

A few years ago I pitched for a client in the grocery
sector. There were only two agencies pitching. It was a
50:50 chance. Our agency met the client 12 times in
14 days. The other company met them only once before
the actual pitch presentation. Who do you think knew
more about the client? Who do you think found out what
the client wanted? Who do you think won? **See the
client as often as is humanly possible.**

A salutary tale

In a pitch for a huge metropolitan transport authority we
had three weeks to come up with the answer to the brief.
We were granted a one-hour session with the senior
client a week before the final pitch presentation. It was a
disastrous meeting. But it was also a brilliant meeting.

The point of the meeting was to test nine potential
strategic options we had identified, to see which ones the
senior client liked and disliked. Each strategy had a chart
of pros and a chart of cons. Within two minutes this
client was staring out of the window, completely
disengaged. On we plowed, pros and cons, strategy
after strategy.

What did we learn? He was a "What's the bottom line?" kind of guy. He wanted the answer, he wanted it quick, and he didn't want to see the workings in the margin.

A week later we went back. We opened by promising that he would see the core strategic thought in one minute and the creative solution 45 seconds after that. We got to the bottom line fast. Every other pitching company trailed through acres of market analysis, research, and team organograms. We won. By a landslide.

If I'm a duck, go "quack"

Finding out what makes the client tick means you'll pitch to the client in the appropriate way. If they use sales terminology, don't use fluffy language; use sales terminology to demonstrate you are like them. If they have a collegiate corporate culture, act like you've just come from the senior common room. Flash, cuff-shooting sales animals will hit the mark with Bloomberg and miss by a mile with Reuters. And vice versa.

Mind your language. We once pitched for a very large information company and described ourselves as "brand architects" in our first slide. After a one-hour presentation our first question came from the Swiss chairman of the company: "Did you build the new Sony HQ in New York?" We had confused the client by trying to be too clever. We were a branding consultancy and he thought we were architects.

Ensure that your team mirrors and complements the client's team. What is the gender mix? The ethnic mix?

The age balance? Is the client suited, or informal? If it's informal, your team of stuffed shirts won't swing it (unless, of course, you've found out that they think they need stuffed shirts for this particular brief). Pitching for Apple should be an entirely different experience from pitching to HSBC.

The purpose of the time before the actual presentation is to find out what the client is like. Everything else you do must stem from this knowledge.

Finding out what makes them tick

Ask ...!

> What are the key issues for your business?

> What keeps you up at night?

> What would success look like in two years' time?

> What do you hate most about agencies/lawyers/ management consultants, etc.?

> What are you looking for in an agency/lawyer/ management consultant, etc.?

> When can we meet your other agencies/advisers?

> What makes you unique as a company, and what do you do that your customers find so valuable?

> What are your key business indicators?

> What do you expect from our company that's different from our competitors?

> What concerns do you have with our company?

> Is there anything we haven't asked that we should be asking?

Increasingly, the client community has introduced a second "voice" with a vote on the outcome of your pitch: **the purchasing (or procurement) specialist**. These people speak a different language from the day-to-day client, and they are looking for different things. Their world is the world of detail. They are excited by process, systems, measurability, and delivery. Their job is to extract from your company the maximum value for their client. Embrace them. Include them. They are not going to go away. Court them as you would court the day-to-day client. But they need courting differently.

Purchasing specialists speak numbers. You must put someone in a lead role with them who is numerate. They are analytical. Your person must be methodical, ordered, and logical. They are fastidious. Your person must dot the i's and cross the t's. They need massive comfort that your company will deliver and be accountable. Make the effort to reassure them through case studies, provable results, cost–benefit analysis. Don't try to dazzle them with showmanship or flashy, colorful presentations. They will not be impressed. Present them with documents that are simple, black and white, with clear explanations. Use the document to demonstrate your professionalism, expertise, and thoroughness. Pre-plan and rehearse every interaction with these people. You will win them over and you will win their very valuable vote.

Doing this just helps you couch your idea, your solution, in a way that has the greatest chance of being understood by the client. It puts your thinking into their language. It helps them to get it. It removes any distractions that

HOW NOT TO COME SECOND

could get in the way. If you're as good as you think you are, that's doing your great ideas a genuine service. And, in turn, doing the client a service as well.

And remember, look after the intermediary. There are specialized experts who know their way around your professional world and who are trusted by the client community to help them draw up shortlists of companies that should be invited to pitch. They might also sit with the client during the pitches and advise them on which company to appoint. As mentioned in chapter 10, ensure you know these people too—inform them about what you are doing, and ask for their perspective on the client. Their intelligence can make all the difference.

To evaluate how best to engage with all these audiences, it's useful to look at a system that can differentiate between personality types and that will give you a practical way of working out how best to communicate with each person on your client's pitch panel. This is the realm of personality profiling.

Personality profiling

In Monty Python's *Life of Brian*, Brian opens the shutters of his bedroom to find hundreds of his "disciples" waiting outside the house to hear his wise words. Trying to get rid of them, he tells them that he is not the Messiah, that they are mistaken and that they don't need anyone to tell them what to do. They must make their own decisions. He implores them to realize that "You are all individuals!" In unison, acting as a mob, they all mindlessly repeat "Yes— we are all individuals!" They have missed Brian's point.

44

It is a truism to say we are all individuals, and yet how useful would it be if you had a quick way to categorize all these individuals into simple archetypes? If you had a way to know how they think, how they like to be treated and how they prefer to be handled? That'd be pretty useful, wouldn't it?

Well, such systems exist. And they are really useful for pitching.

There are many very well-documented psychological tests to identify the different behavioral styles that people have. The system I prefer divides all people into four major archetypes and I have found it of great use in designing how best to present to different clients. The system can be applied to individuals, to teams, and, I believe, to organizations. It can show the dominant style at work in an organization—both your own as the pitching company and that of the client organization.

The system is designed around a very simple questionnaire that asks the individual to choose between a set of alternative descriptors in evaluating that person's strengths and weaknesses. The answers are then transferred on to a master analysis that reveals that person's dominant style of behavior.

In very simple terms, this system divides the world into those who are people-oriented and those who are task-oriented. Within these two categories, there are those who prefer to operate at speed and who work fast, and those who prefer to take their time and work at a slower pace.

What you end up with is four archetypes: Expressives and Amiables, who are more **people**-oriented, and Drivers and Analyticals, who are more focused on the **task**.

Between the Expressives and the Amiables, the Expressives operate fast, and the Amiables like to take their time.

On the other side, the Drivers work quickly and the Analyticals are much slower and more deliberate.

Knowing what type you are, and what type your clients may be, is immensely helpful in determining the style of your pitch.

Why?

Pitching is really just a super-advanced communication technique. And the core skills of great communicators are to "know thyself," to use the senses to pick up response signals from others, and the ability to **adapt behavior to develop better rapport with an audience**.

This personality profiling gives you the information you need to adapt your behavior with people who are different from you, and so get on with them better. And if you get on with them better, they will receive your presentation more effectively. You will be able to pitch to them in the language and style they find most comfortable.

A note to all those cynics out there. Is this manipulation? Am I asking you to abandon your own personality and become chameleon-like? No. I am only interested in helping you to get your message across effectively. No one can escape their own personality—nor should they want to. It's just that by being aware of other people's personality styles you can avoid destructive personality clashes that will get in the way of winning the business.

A pen portrait of the four personality types

How they see themselves

There is often a marked disparity between the way we see ourselves and the way other people perceive us. Here is how the four different types see themselves.

Expressives Energetic, creative, open, optimistic, and quick on their feet. They are easily bored and don't like detail. They need to be stimulated and enjoy the limelight.

Amiables Warm, accepting, patient, cooperative, friendly, and unconfrontational. They like to build consensus (slowly) and are very good at building long-term relationships.

Drivers Exacting, efficient, determined, direct, and decisive. They have little time for social niceties and want to get on with it. They hate debates that go around and around and they want to get it sorted.

Analyticals Analytical, precise, careful, reserved, and logical. They will not be hurried, they make decisions based on fact and evidence, not supposition and hunch. They don't like showiness. In a political election they will vote according to policy issues, not personalities.

How others see them

The effect these four groups have on people who are not like them can be alarming.

Expressives People who are not Expressives tend to see them as pushy, superficial, prone to exaggerate, with no follow-through, and overconfident. Expressives are especially irritating to Analyticals, because they are so emotive. Expressives fizz about and fall in love with the last great idea they hear about. They are naturally enthusiastic. Expressives believe they are the ideas brigade. If it wasn't for them there'd be no new ideas. They are life's natural entrepreneurs.

Amiables Amiables can often be viewed as weak, time-wasting (all that touchy-feely small talk before getting down to business), lacking goals, and slow to make decisions. Amiables irritate the hell out of Drivers. But Amiables can knit relationships together and tend to look at the long term.

Drivers These are usually seen by the other groups as being autocratic, critical, demanding, insensitive, and domineering. (Please note, Drivers can't see much wrong with any of these adjectives and might actually be quite proud of being like this!) If you get two Drivers trying to run a meeting, you're in trouble. They'll both be competing with each other for control of the room. Drivers believe that if it wasn't for them nothing would ever get done. Everyone else would just keep talking around and around the task at hand. Drivers make things happen.

Analyticals These tend to be seen (especially by Expressives) as stubborn, nit picking, perfectionist, pedantic, and unemotional. Again, this type of person would wear such labels with pride. After all, if they didn't dot the i's and cross the t's, who would? Other groups find their pace excruciatingly leaden.

Concerns and dislikes of each style

Expressives Hate bureaucracy, slow progress, people who show no interest or enthusiasm, too much detail, negative attitudes. Expressives are easy to spot. They like being in the spotlight, are straight out with their opinions, and present their ideas with emotion not with facts.

Amiables Don't hate things, but they're not very keen on conflict, uncooperative people, aggressive behavior, people who set out to hurt other's feelings, or egotistical individualists (they're team players). Their offices will have pictures of family and other personal memorabilia and they need to be eased in to business with small talk (they want to get to know you first). Drivers beware! These people need to be seduced. If you move too rapidly to business, they will feel you have intellectually mugged them!

Drivers Loathe anyone displaying a lack of interest, disagreement (with their point of view), time-wasting, indecision, and delays. Drivers will go home at night and leave an entirely clean desk. They are obsessed with lists (to do) and will instantly judge you as ineffectual if you do not produce an agenda for the meeting within seconds of sitting down. If your office is a mess, they will be less inclined to do business with you and will take it as evidence that you are unprepared.

Analyticals Find loud, opinionated people uncomfortable to be around. They do not like too much "creativity" (they dislike colorful charts, for example, unless there is a solid logical reason for the use of color) and find illogical thinking very irritating. They are unforgiving of factual errors or a lack of evidence to support recommendations. Analyticals prefer documents to dialog. (Working documents keep things formal and give focus to a presentation.) They also like to use desks or tables as a physical barrier to prevent intimacy. Another Analytical trait is an overfondness for using big, complicated words to convey precise meaning. They would rather ask for "dialog and technical interaction based on fact and evidence" than the simpler "straight talking."

Many "people-oriented" people find Analyticals very difficult to fathom.

But Analyticals are becoming increasingly influential in deciding the outcome of pitches because they are often the people who hold the purse strings— either as finance director or as purchasing and procurement director. It is therefore worth spending a little time looking at some Dos and Don'ts specifically for them.

When presenting to Analyticals:

DO:

> Send them an agenda in advance, and confirm the time and date of the meeting.
> Be prepared with evidence of accuracy and quality.
> Be practical.
> Be logical and ordered.
> List the pros and cons.
> Use step-by-step timetables.
> Minimize the risk for them.
> Stick to business.
> Show them how the solution will work.
> Take your time.
> Be persistent, but not too persistent.
> Be direct but low pressure. They will not be hurried or bamboozled into a decision.

DON'T:

> Be disorganized, messy, casual, loud.
> Be unrealistic with deadlines.
> Be vague.
> Offer personal incentives.
> Threaten.
> Forget to take notes.

A lawyer friend of mine made a pitch to a predominantly analytical group of people. He talked about the importance of collaboration, of cross-disciplinary synergy, and of systems to ensure control of process, quality of output, and consistency. As my friend left the client, he bumped into his colleagues from the Manchester office. They were next on to present. Neither office knew the other was pitching. This put the lie to everything he'd just been saying about systems that prevent the left hand not knowing what the right hand is doing. The client was there too, and witnessed the encounter. Based on this evidence, the client didn't give my friend the business. Nor did he give it to my friend's colleagues from Manchester.

A last thought about personality types

You have to be wary of over-reliance on these sorts of tools. Of course, we are all individuals, and most people will be a combination of two, three, or even four of the personality types outlined above. Additionally, you are unlikely to be able to get your prospective client to fill in the questionnaire every time you do a pitch. However, familiarize yourself with the

> You'll soon be able to discover intuitively what language and style will work best.

telltale signs and apply the methodology to your pitches and you will soon be able to discover intuitively what language and style will work best with each client organization. And that type of knowledge is invaluable in helping you beat your competitors. If you're interested in finding out more, just type in *expressives*, *drivers*, *amiables*, and *analyticals* on any internet search engine and you'll be spoilt for choice.

Chapter 12
Solve the problem

Presumably you are good at this. It is the technical expertise that the client needs, your craft skill. Your knowledge of the law. Your architectural expertise. Your ability to generate publicity. Your analytical prowess. Your skill at customer relationship management, at design, or digital media. And this is, as far as you are concerned, the interesting bit. The knotty problem that you pride yourself on being able to solve. It is also where you will, if you are not careful, lose the pitch.

Why?

Because you like this bit, because it plays to your strengths, because it is inside your comfort zone. You will spend the vast majority of your time on this section—to the detriment of the other sections that will actually (in combination with a great solution to the problem) deliver victory.

The whole effort of the pitch team must be harnessed to deliver the *most* right solution *most* quickly. This is where your efficiency in using the available time will come into play. Far too many "close second" pitches expend far too much time finessing and worrying away at the technical solution to the client's problem. In order to maximize your chances of winning the pitch, this entire process needs to be compressed into as short a timeframe as possible.

From initial brief to final presentation, about 60% of your time should be devoted to coming up with the actual solution. The balance of time should be invested in getting to know the client (face to face wherever possible: see chapter 11), rehearsing (more about this in chapter 14), and getting the team to act and think like a team.

All of this means that pitching teams need to arrive at the **most right solution** quicker than they usually do. You cannot afford the luxury of finessing the solution to the nth degree, right up to the last moment. Here are some practical tools to **accelerate the process of solution generation**.

1 Use the available time wisely

Know how long you have and plan in all the other activities you must perform. Whatever is left over is your *thinking* time. Be efficient with how you use it. Have one person who worries over the client brief all the time, keeps coming back to it, and ensures that the core team answers every single item on the brief.

2 Use the best brains in your company

Gray-hairs have experience. They have seen many problems; they will have seen your client's problem before, albeit in another guise. Their experience will help you take short cuts, eliminate making basic mistakes and wasting time chasing after impractical solutions. They will help you go 70% of the way to the most right solution. Get them together 24 hours after issuing them with the client's brief and you will have cracked most of the hard intellectual work in the first two days of your allotted time.

If you have very bright sparks in your company, get them in to this session as well. They may come up with the creative thinking that will help distinguish your solution from your competitors'. They may see an angle no one else will see. They will have the **objectivity of ignorance** of the client's business that occasionally yields genius and opens the door to possibilities everyone else is too involved with the problem to see. Use these people: they can mine gold for you.

3 Use Six-Hat Thinking

With plaudits to Edward De Bono (the man who brought the world lateral thinking), this is a technique that helps you deconstruct the client's issues so that you can tackle the problem from specific angles rather than as one indigestible whole.

The team members don six colored hats, in sequence:

White for fact and data. What do we know from the information we have? What do we need to find out? Here, you analyze from past trends.

Red for emotion and feelings. What do I feel about this client and this issue? What does my gut instinct have to say about this? Nothing needs to be supported by fact or logic—this is about getting the intuitive elements into play.

Black for pessimism. What is the worst that can happen to this client company? What are the contingency plans? What risks are attached to our solution?

Yellow for optimism. What can be gained from acting now or implementing our recommended course of action? What will be the upsides?

Green for fresh. What completely fresh insights do we have for this client? What lateral thoughts can be brought to bear?

Blue for sky, the overview. Bring all the other elements, all the other thoughts and ideas produced in the previous colored-hat discussions, and sift through them to produce an overall picture. This synthesis will be your solution template. It may not produce the exact right answer, but using this method will ensure robust discussion and a thorough analysis of all the aspects of the client's situation and your company's approach to solving that situation.

4 Write a logic chain

All your thoughts and ideas need to be condensed and ordered. A truly useful tool is the logic chain. This is a single piece of paper on which is written the skeleton of your overall argument. It is a **series of sequential statements** that:

> articulate the client's central issue
> list the core reasons for this situation
> describe the desired outcome

> describe your hypothesis for remedy and your reasons for this remedy

> anticipate the results of taking this action

> articulate how it will be measured for effectiveness.

All through the pitch period, this logic chain acts as your guide. It will change over the course of your investigations, as your thinking develops and as you discover new information on your client. Once it is as good as it can get, you will hang your presentation around it and it will also serve as the backbone of your **management summary**.

5 Test your hypotheses

Use the time you have to try out your ideas and logic on a number of valuable constituencies that can help you mold and refine the thinking.

Do anything you can to torture-test your viewpoint.

These include **dispassionate colleagues, focus groups, third-party individuals with specific expertise**, and, of course, **the clients**. Do anything you can to torture-test your viewpoint. Not just for logic and technical merit, but also for how it will play to the client—especially if there are "political" reasons why the solution will, or will not, work for your client and any other "softer" issues surrounding your answer. You don't want anything to get in the way—make sure you **minimize the risk** of this happening.

Chapter 13
Price properly

If you remember back to chapter 8, *Seven ready-made excuses for coming a close second*, number 6 was "They think we are too expensive." Don't get me wrong, price is going to be a factor in the client's decision to appoint, but it's your job to make price as irrelevant to the decision as you can. Mediocre pitchers genuinely believe that price is *the* determining factor in the client's decision on whom to appoint.

Price appropriately

Presumably, if you're good at what you do, you'll be charging a premium for doing it. And let's face it, you're always going to be more expensive than your competitors. But you are also going to provide better value. You do need to get the pricing appropriate, but you also need to put the price in context.

Usually you know if you're in the frame to win if, very soon after you've pitched, the client wants to talk money. If you haven't heard, then the client is probably favoring another company and you're headed for a "close second" call.

Sometimes—rarely—the client will appoint on the spot and you have to be prepared for the matter of what you'll charge. I remember making a pitch in Sweden for a product that helped with tobacco-withdrawal symptoms. There were only three of us from our company, and only three people from the clients. In this pitch meeting they had visibly "fallen in love" with our strategist. We'd knocked their socks off and they asked us, "How much if we could agree right now and you walk out of here with the business?" We stipulated the figure and they agreed. Immediately. This is the most perfect illustration I've ever experienced of making price a non-issue.

Nowadays, all companies that offer professional services experience tough negotiations with client procurement departments. Don't be fazed. Recently, I met a very senior lawyer who specialized in European employment law. He recounted how he'd been asked to "pop down the corridor" by his potential client to tie up the details of his contract with the Head of Procurement. Our lawyer duly popped down the corridor and knocked on the procurement chief's door. "Come in and sit down," growled the procurer, without even lifting his eyes from the papers on his desk. "Before we even start this conversation I want an immediate agreement from you that you'll cut your hourly charge by at least 15%—or else there won't be any further conversation."

Quietly, our lawyer, who'd been taking his papers out of his briefcase, started to put them all back. He moved to stand up and said, "I'm so sorry, I totally misunderstood what this conversation was all about. I thought it was about preventing your company from losing a potential 1.2 million euros in an action brought by three of your former staff. I didn't realize it was about saving 98 euros an hour. I'm obviously not what you're looking for. I'll be on my way."

This rather threw the procurement chief. He'd been instructed to appoint this lawyer, and to do so on favorable terms. He was now totally on the back foot. He had mistaken price for value—our lawyer friend had just reminded him of the difference.

The moral of the story? Hold your nerve, remember that they want your services and your team (otherwise they wouldn't be having this conversation with you, would they?), and take every opportunity to remind them of the quality of the outcome rather than the cost of the input. You are not selling a commodity. You are selling decades of accumulated expertise. If one of your competitors has dropped their trousers on the price and is looking to "buy" the business, let them. They'll lose money on it and word will get around. And in a few months' time you can call the client and check if it's all working out. It won't be.

Know your value

Another illustration of the power of appropriate pricing is a story about the painter Whistler. In his famous libel case against Ruskin in 1878, Whistler was challenged about his fee of 200 guineas for a painting that took him only two days to complete from scratch. "I ask [200 guineas] for the knowledge I have gained in the work of a lifetime," was his defense. He wasn't charging by the hour for the job at hand but for the wisdom and experience he brought to the task; he was charging for his ability, competency, and specialized skill, not for his time.

Just as Whistler's work was worth more than the time it took him to perform the task, you too can perform tasks because you have accumulated years of experience and reputation.

Charge for your wisdom, not for your hours.

Whistler knew his value. Know yours. Be realistic, be responsible, and calculate a rigorous defense of your value. But however you arrive at your proposal—time based, value pricing, commissions, cost plus—your fees must obviously be in the competitive range, with an explicable margin. It is your job to present the recommendation of your fees as **true value for money** (by your definition and according to your real costs), and to show the pricing proposal to be cost-effective for the client.

When you are selling professional services it is usually difficult to isolate your company's contribution from all the other factors affecting the end result of the project. But if you *can* demonstrate a real cost–benefit were the client to use your company, make sure it's front and center in your pitch. It is said that some media-buying operations—those organizations that purchase TV airtime, or newspaper space, on behalf of clients—have demonstrated the savings they can make to a client's media budget by taking in suitcases of banknotes to the value of the savings! The purpose is to show physically what a large amount of money can be saved—to bring to large and immediate life what is otherwise a single line of figures on a spreadsheet.

Share the risks and the rewards

If you can, it is also sensible to incorporate a **performance-related** component into your pricing proposal. Apart from anything else, this signals a mutual coincidence of interest—a willingness to share risk and reward. It signals your shared ambition for the client's business. Such a scheme could be predicated on a combination of hard and soft measures but it must rely on rigorous monitoring of results and an honest evaluation at the end of the project.

As most clients are interested not in **inputs** or **outputs** but in **outcomes**, the largest component of your performance-based component should be tied to the success of the client company. It is often a good starting point to find out how your potential clients earn their bonus and use that as the model. More qualitative measures—such as the client's rating of your company's overall level of service, responsiveness, and knowledge of their business—could also be incorporated to provide a bonus to your remuneration. But the basic principle is to share risk and reward: you put a proportion of your profit at risk in order to gain a potentially greater reward if you hit pre-agreed performance targets.

Price with pride

You may well rehearse your main presentation but I'll bet you don't **rehearse your fee presentation**. And this is where the real money will be made! Often a separate presentation is held just to discuss the terms of engagement. Like the regular pitch, this needs to be planned methodically.

> Where will the meeting take place?

> When will it occur in the overall sequence of the pitch process?

> Who will be present from the client side? What do you know about their team? What's their form? What are they looking to achieve?

> What are the issues of contention about your pricing and service proposal?

You need to prepare thoroughly for this "pitch." You need all the facts and figures to justify your argument, all the appropriate information. And you need to know what price shifts you can afford, or are willing, to make—and in return for what concessions from your client.

Your pricing proposal will need to be documented thoroughly. The type of person likely to be evaluating your proposal will prefer plain, factual documents (an Analytical: see chapter 11). Bald facts rather than hyperbolic claims. Black and white rather than color. They will want chapter and verse on why your proposal is as it is—evidence of proper calculation, evidence of your proven ability to deliver results. They will want to negotiate with people who understand what they are talking about, who speak their language (numbers), and are experienced in fee negotiation.

Often, the client will say your fees are 25% more expensive than anyone else's. Maybe they are. It is your job to explain why you are worth it. Be patient. Be calm.

Explain. Don't be panicked or browbeaten—they will use emotion to try to make you capitulate. Remain rational. You are worth the price difference. When my father-in-law, David, was at school as an eight-year-old, one of his school masters came across him being pummeled by a much bigger, older boy. The larger boy had David pinned to the ground and was hitting him repeatedly in the face. When the teacher appeared, David remembers thinking, "Thank goodness for that. Now I'm saved." But instead of pulling the larger boy off and reprimanding him, the teacher stood over them both and said to David:

DON'T BE BULLIED!

David went on to captain the England rugby team, so it turned out to be good advice! When you are negotiating on price, don't be bullied. It's difficult to give good advice from a bended knee position, and it's difficult to respect someone who won't stick up for himself. Here's an example. A client once reacted to our pricing policy with the exclamation: "HOW MUCH?!"

"I know. Astoundingly good value, isn't it?" was our reply.

Price with pride. They'll respect you in the morning.

Chapter 14
Practice

Great champions at any endeavor know that practice, practice, practice makes perfect. **The "hard yards" are the ones done out of the glare of public performance.** If you're a footballer, they are the hours, days, weeks, and months devoted to going out there and honing your goal-kicking technique in a muddy field in the middle of winter in the rain.

Alongside being organized and getting to know the client, it is this—**the self-discipline to practice**—that makes the biggest difference between coming first and coming nowhere in pitching.

When I tell people that they should **rehearse three times** before any pitch, they look at me like I don't live in the real world. They are too busy to rehearse once, let alone three times. They are "**busy fools**." They are too busy running from one emergency to the next to concentrate on what is important rather than merely urgent. They are the ones who get the "you came a close second" call over and over again. They are the ones being amateur in a world of professionals.

Why rehearse?

A very large client in the beauty business came in to a public relations agency to hear their pitch for one of her products. The PR team had the projector on, charts ready to go. The client reached over to the projector and switched it off. "Talk to me," she said. "Show me what you've found out and what you think we should do." The managing director of the PR company hadn't rehearsed and didn't know what the pitch was about. He was speechless—he was caught without a point of view.

This is only a horror story if you're one of those people who rely on PowerPoint to remind you why you're in the room and what you're going to say. Would your team be able to present your pitch if the client did that to you? Or, like millions of amateur pitchers, do you cram your PowerPoint charts with words, to act as a script of what to say?

True pitch champions rehearse three times because this is where the **magic** comes. This is where, to be frank, great technique can compensate for shortcomings in content or, even better, make great content really shine.

Why three times?

The first rehearsal, let's be frank, isn't really a rehearsal. Everyone comes into the room, you lay out your scribbled charts or put a draft presentation up on the screen, and you plod through the content. What you are doing is **checking the sense**, not rehearsing. An old boss of mine used to refer to this as the "Edward Scissorhands" stage: a cut-and-paste as you change, delete, move, and add in order to get the shape and content of your presentation into some kind of logical order. After two hours of this, the team leader divvies up the roles in a very casual manner. ("I'll do the intro, you do the first bit up to here, then hand over to Fred for the next section, and back to me, I hand on to Maria …")

Then everyone leaves the room and the team leader says, "Great everybody, good rehearsal!" **But no one has rehearsed!**

Those who think themselves very professional go for a **second rehearsal**. Having re-briefed all the presenters to edit their charts, the leader gathers the team for a run-through. At this stage all the presenters are stutteringly familiar with their bit of the overall presentation (by no means perfectly prepared, but they know roughly what they want to say). In the few hours that have been stolen from their day jobs to do this second run-through, each presenter does their bit but then takes any comments and goes off either to amend their section or to tend to other business. So none of the team sees the whole presentation—they concentrate purely on their own bit. **And we all know what happens when a bunch of individual performers come together—they lose to the people who act like a team.**

The third rehearsal is where you produce the magic. By now the presentation makes sense. It has been pared down to its shortest, most logical, and compelling expression. Everyone knows their bit. Everyone is familiar with the important parts of their own section. And in the third rehearsal it all comes together as one seamless flow of brilliance.

People buy conviction. Clients want certainty and fluency. They want clever, innovative solutions delivered in a convincing, dynamic way. They want bright people who spark off each other, respect each other and who clearly get excited by their own well-thought-through ideas. This is the purpose of the third rehearsal—**to sell your idea by making the clients fall in love with your team**. How do you do this?

In your third rehearsal you must focus on those "soft" areas that send powerful but intangible signals to your client that they want to see, feel, and hear. They want to buy a team, so you rehearse behaving like a team. They want to buy people with whom they will enjoy working, so you rehearse how they will be infected with your team's enthusiasm. They want answers to their problem, so you strip away anything that gets in the way of them understanding what it is you are asking them to buy. You deliver it in clean, crisp, uncluttered language, and get to the point quickly. They want people who understand them and share their ambition for the business, so **make them feel their mission is as important as sending a man to the moon**. And they want to see brilliance, so make them spectators at the birth of a great idea.

To look like a team, make your handovers between speakers interesting and smooth. Most presenters get to the end of their section and say, "I will now hand you over to my colleague ..." (showing they don't know the person's name) "... who will talk you through our strategic recommendations."

At this point, the unrehearsed person up next shuffles their papers together and hesitantly gets to their feet, emitting a squeak as they do so because their larynx isn't warmed up. (They also spent the last five minutes frantically scribbling last-minute notes on their crib sheets, so they missed their cue.) It doesn't look very teamy. How much better, then, that you rehearse to effect a handover that looks spontaneous?

For example: "We conducted six research groups. Two in Scandinavia, one in France, and three in South East Asia. At the groups we found three very interesting types of reaction to your service. In South East Asia … well, Maria, you were at the groups in Singapore, tell us what happened." Maria, who knew this was coming because they'd practiced it in the third rehearsal, immediately kicks in with her comments. She can then segue into the rest of the research or she can bat it to and fro with the main presenter. Doesn't sound like much, but it signals teamwork and fluency. It signals a like-minded bunch of people who can converse easily, who have all been intimately involved in the process and who, vitally, **spark off each other**. And, of course, you can't do this if you haven't rehearsed because if Maria doesn't know the presenter is coming to her, she'll be caught out and the whole presentation will grind to a halt.

Choose good presenters

Rehearsal has other benefits in addition to getting the team familiar with the content. The American comedian Steve Martin has a lovely saying:

> Some people have a way with words, other people not have way.

Rehearsals weed out the presenters who will damage rather than enhance your pitch presentation. People who "not have way" don't get to present. It's that simple. Just because Freddie has worked like a beaver and really deserves a speaking role in the actual pitch doesn't mean he should present. If Freddie is useless at presenting, Freddie doesn't present. You only get one shot at this, it's too important. No one will thank you for coming second because you were too nice, so

BE RUTHLESS!

There is an apocryphal tale about a truly gifted, delightfully funny, highly original art director. He produced a lot of the most internationally awarded, affectionately remembered advertising for some of the best-known brands in Britain. He was also useless for anything after midday because he drank. A lot.

One day, he created an ad campaign for a well-known brand. He wanted to present his ideas personally. But the meeting was scheduled for 3:00 pm. The man running the pitch knew that by 3:00 pm this particular art director would be drunk and troublesome. He banned the art director from presenting.

The art director pleaded his case: "I won't be badly behaved. I want this campaign to run. It'll be famous. Only I can present this work and make them see it, how fantastic it will be!" he cried.

The answer kept coming back: "No." Eventually, the man running the pitch told our art director why he wouldn't be presenting.

"This client has a rather large nose. I know you. You'll stagger in, drunk, and you won't be able to resist making a comment about his proboscis."

"I won't, I won't," protested the art director. "I'll be good as gold. I want this campaign to run! I'll be good as gold."

The pitch leader relented.

The pitch day came. The 3:00 pm meeting started. No art director. Half an hour into the meeting, he spilled into the room, very drunk, giggling. He walked straight up to the client, grabbed the client's nose between two fingers, shook it and ran from the room laughing uncontrollably.

We need genius. Genius is very difficult to manage. But manage it you must. Be ruthless!

The Pitch-Meister

Rehearsal also allows you to play to the presentational styles of your team members. To vary the pace, alter the cadence, vary the emphasis. And iron out behavioral quirks. If your CEO is using inappropriate language, uses clichés, keeps repeating phrases or making unconscious body movements, now is the time to make him aware of what impression he is making. This is why you need a senior **"Pitch-Meister"** in the rehearsal who has the experience and seniority to be objective and point out issues to the team members, however senior they are.

Every successful pitch machine has one of these. In your rehearsals you need the objectivity of ignorance—the view of someone outside the team. Unencumbered by the details, this person can see the flaws in the team's arguments, the chemistry between them, what will play well and what won't. A great Pitch-Meister will edit, prune, and hone your pitch presentation to perfection. All those overwordy charts, those mediocre ideas, those weak arguments, that confusing technical jargon will be exposed by the experienced objective listener. Better now, to a friend, than later to the client. The Pitch-Meister will give your presentation the panache, the punchiness, the structure, and the force of argument to make it convincing and compelling.

Practice your techniques

Listen supportively

Unprofessional pitchers are only concerned with their bit of the presentation. Because they are so disorganized and have thrown together the presentation at the last minute, they are amending their script right up to the moment they get to their feet. And when, after stumbling and stammering their way through their bit (the best they aspire to is "to get away with it" rather than to sparkle with brilliance), they sit down, spent, you can see them mentally disengage from the meeting. I've even seen one member of a so-called team present his bit, sit down, and swivel his chair 180 degrees, turning his back to the client and the rest of his team. He began examining the pictures on the wall. He was, in effect, saying to

everyone: "There, I've done my bit and I was brilliant.
If this lot screw up, don't blame me." We came a close
second; lack of team spirit was cited as a reason.

I'm not asking you to stare bug-eyed with fascination at
every word that emanates from your colleagues' mouths.
I am saying that each member of the team must look
engaged and interested in the overall show. Because every
client panel is
watching the pitching
team's body language
to see how they
interact together. And
if you're not interested
in what you've got to say, why should the client be
interested? It's another thing you need to practice so that
you come over as a real team.

> Each member of the team must look engaged and interested.

Pitch on a postcard

This is a superb discipline. In your rehearsal, the Pitch-
Meister must ensure that every presenter can write down
on the back of a postcard the one thing the client *must*
understand by the time that presenter sits down. It forces
people to focus on what's important. It stops presenters
waffling. It is a self-editing tool to sharpen your
presentation and it ensures each section of the
presentation has a point.

Tell a story

Humankind has gathered around campfires for tens of
thousands of years and been entertained by storytellers.

When you attend a wedding, watch the body language of the audience when the Best Man starts his speech with "I'd like to begin by telling you a story."

Everyone will relax and sit back, ready to enjoy the tale. We like stories. We like people who tell us good stories. We flock to the movies in droves because we can't resist a good story. Think how the wedding guests would react if our Best Man stood up and announced that he'd like to present a case study? Not quite as enticing, is it? Not such an attractive proposition.

What sort of story should you tell? Tell a story that is real, that is personal to you and to your audience. That is believable. That uses references they can relate to. That can be repeated. I once pitched for a jeans manufacturer who prided themselves on the fact that their jeans were as well made as the brand leader but "more honestly" priced. They felt that the market had run away with itself and that customers were being taken for a ride. At the end of the pitch we read them an extract from a book by Anita Roddick, founder of The Body Shop:

I am still looking for the modern day equivalent of those Quakers who ran successful businesses, made money because they offered honest products and treated their people decently, worked hard, spent honestly, saved honestly, gave honest value for money, put back more than they took out and told no lies. This business creed, sadly, seems long forgotten.

Anita Roddick, *Body & Soul*, 1991, Ebury Press, London

We told the story of how we had stumbled across this extract and how it triggered the solution we had shown them earlier in the presentation. We said—and we believed—that it was hugely inspiring to represent such an honest-value brand, a brand that didn't overprice. And we let them feel our own values chimed with this philosophy. The story told them something about us, as we told it to reveal something about them. It helped them see us as kindred spirits, and as the right business partner for them.

Once, when pitching to a directory services client, we ended with a story that told how we, as a team, had come to use the client's service and evangelized about it to friends over the last four weeks. So convinced of the company's future success were we that we all bought a modest amount of shares in the company. In our summary slide of why the client should appoint us, our last point was "We are all stockholders." We brandished our share certificates and we threatened to dump all our stock if they didn't appoint us! This spoke volumes about our team: that we believed in the product (the clients were all stockholders too) and that we had a sense of humor (500 shares "dumped" on the market wasn't going to collapse the share price). The clients were all fairly young and very go-getter. They didn't take themselves too seriously either. It worked and we won.

Speak from the heart, from your own experience. If you've established your technical credentials through the presentation, your own personal experience will only add credibility. Help the client understand that you have seen similar problems and tell them how you tackled them. Tell them what you learned from the experience.

They will appreciate this glimpse into your relevant experience, especially if it's colloquial rather than presentational. "If it were me, this is what I'd do …" is more powerful than the corporate "We recommend you adopt the following course of action …" But it is only more effective if you've demonstrated your credibility through the preceding presentation.

Nasty questions

At the end of the third rehearsal, force the team to sit down and write down the worst question the client

Write down the worst question the client could ask you.

could ask you … because they *will* ask it. Work out what the answer is and who will answer. And make an agreement that **only one extra shot is allowed**. That means, if another person on your team wants to add to the answer given by their colleague (the one you all agreed would answer the question) they can—but no one else can add their bit after that. Otherwise you'll have anarchy.

Then work out the second nastiest question the clients could ask. (Because they will.) And go through the same process.

And so on until you have exhausted the list of potential questions.

Final preparations

Re-read the client's brief. Check you've answered every facet of the brief.

> Is your key message on-brief, clear, buyable, robust, deliverable?

> Is it delivered in a style appropriate to the client and the occasion?

> Will you be memorable? (For the right reasons!)

> What will they remember you for?

> What will the clients feel when they leave the room?

Write the two-page management summary of your presentation. (Refer to your logic chain: chapter 12.)

Chapter 15
Great presentation

When it's time to sing for your supper, remember these golden rules.

1 Control the environment

Wherever you're pitching, **play at home**—make the environment work for you. If you're presenting at the client's offices, go and see the room you'll be presenting in and work out how to use it best. Sketch where all the electrical sockets are, the doors and windows. Is it modern, or oak-paneled? Where will you all sit? Is there an IT specialist on hand? How will you display your work? Can you get in 20 minutes early to set up? Make sure you and your team feel at home, even if you are on the other side of the world. You want to feel in control, so treat yourself and your team well. Get a good night's sleep the night before the pitch. Allow plenty of extra time to get to the client's offices. Remember: **what can go wrong will go wrong**. If the pitch is at 11:30 am in Paris and you're coming in from London, travel the day before. If the Eurostar train out of St Pancras station is delayed on the morning of the pitch, you've had it. Even if you do make it just in time, you'll be sweaty and breathless and anxious, so you won't perform well. Always take a spare shirt for the meeting—changing into a sharply ironed shirt will help you feel more confident and it's useful to have a spare in case you spill anything during breakfast or lunch.

2 Go last

Ask the client if you can pitch last of all. Normally clients are happy to oblige. Going last has several competitive advantages:

a) You get more time to prepare and rehearse your pitch.

b) You will be the last team they see, so their memory of you will be fresher.

c) Most crucially, you can get to the important stuff quicker. By now they will have been subjected to several relatively undifferentiated presentations, with all the laborious market analysis and other non-value-added guff that pitchers think they need to show in order to signal that they have done their homework. You can kick off by saying that **within the first 15 minutes the clients will see the answer to their question**—which is what they are interested in seeing.

3 Look at your office with fresh eyes

Think of **the presentation beyond the four walls** of the room you are presenting in. If the clients are visiting your offices, use the premises to impress. It is a sad fact that we all become **"building blind"** in our own offices. We come in every day and become desensitized to the image our building creates. Clients walk in for the first time and see it all with very keen eyes.

What image do you want to create? Is the client going to be impressed with an atmosphere of business and industry or with contemplative silence? Think about it, don't leave it to chance. If you are pitching at lunchtime, make sure everyone is alerted to stay at their desks—there is little less impressive than ranks of empty desks. One company I know ensures that the moment the lift doors open and a client (or prospective employee) walks into the reception area, they are visually and aurally assaulted with busy-ness and activity. This agency wants to ensure that any spectators feel they are in a happening, stimulating, busy, and successful place. If you watch carefully, you'll probably see that someone strides purposefully through reception in one direction ... and then strides purposefully back in the other direction a few minutes later. It is a show for your benefit. **And like all great shows, it has been carefully choreographed.**

In a famous management consultancy's offices they have an escalator to take you up to the cavernous reception area. Above the escalator is a steel vaulted roof and a cathedral-like atrium made of glass and burnished steel. Behind the reception desk, peopled by two immaculately dressed and unsmiling assistants, is a glass map of the world with all the consultancy's offices around planet earth stenciled on to it. All of this architectural drama is to signal that you are in a place of serious business and intellect (you have to travel up an escalator just to get on to their intellectual level!). How antithetical, then, to see a Mrs Miggins-style tea lady with her trolley of cakes and her big tea urn, resplendent in flowery housecoat and hairnet, trundle along the walkway behind the world map. It rather punctures the grandiosity of the brand promise. But I saw it.

4 Be good hosts

Have a **chief listener** on your team—a senior person whose role is to watch and listen in order to ensure the clients are understanding everything you are saying and to feel the effect your presentation is creating. They can stop the presentation to summarize or clarify. They also act as ringmaster and host. They control the tempo of the meeting and must be sensitive to the client team's need to break or rest. In short, they are there to steer proceedings smoothly and to make the experience comfortable.

5 Take a break

NEVER present for more than one hour (preferably 45 minutes) without some sort of break.

6 Don't play musical chairs

NEVER have more than five presenters in that hour (or you will be up and down on your feet so fast the client will lose the thread of what you are saying).

7 Keep it simple

Your audience cannot absorb tons of information in one hour. Presenting is a bit like playing catch. If you stand three meters away from me and I throw you two great handfuls of sweets, how many will you catch? I can tell you: one or maybe two, but probably none. Our brains just cannot cope with loads of objects flying toward us—it doesn't know where to focus and where to direct its attention. If I throw you only one sweet, 99 times out of 100 you will catch it. Think of each point you are trying to make as one sweet. If you throw your audience too many, they will miss all of them in a blur of words and charts. Limit the number of key points you want to make. (This is where the **pitch on a postcard**, mentioned in the last chapter, is so useful.)

The other advantage of pruning your presentation into a few key points is that weak arguments reduce the power of strong arguments. They dilute the impact of your key messages. Use your Pitch-Meister to weed out these distracting elements.

> Keep the main thing the main thing.

8 It's a show

So make it entertaining. Like all shows, it must have a beginning, a middle, and an end.

The beginning

Make the beginning compelling—exciting, interesting, and memorable. Tell the clients what they are about to enjoy (think of the narrator in a play, setting the scene). Probably the most famous start to a very big pitch is the brave opening taken by a company called ABM when they pitched for the British Rail business. At that time, British Rail was an appalling mess. The rolling stock was old and decrepit; the staff were surly and belligerent; the trains ran late, and were dirty and unpleasant to travel in.

Overall, the experience for British Rail's customers was ghastly.

The story goes that the senior management team of British Rail turned up at the appointed time to see ABM's pitch. When they entered reception, instead of being greeted by a smiling and friendly receptionist, they were ignored while the receptionist finished a private telephone conversation and then went back to studying her magazine. Eventually, she looked up and said, "Yes? Whadya' want?"

The chairman of British Rail was rather taken aback by this. He was used to being treated deferentially by everyone he met. He composed himself and said that he and his other board members had come for a meeting with the ABM team. "First I've heard of it," piped the receptionist. "Hang on, I'll see if they're in."

She indicated to the board members to take a seat. The seats were hard and uncomfortable. The table in the middle of the reception area was chipped and tatty. Newspapers were scattered around, half-read and crumpled. Some of them were weeks old. The ashtrays spilled over with cigarette butts and days of accumulated ash. The clients sat down and quietly seethed. After waiting for another 20 minutes, they'd had enough. The chairman flew to his feet and marched over to the receptionist, who was engaged on yet another personal call.

"WHAT IS GOING ON?" bellowed the chairman. "I've had just about enough of this. Is someone coming to get us or not?" On that cue, the ABM pitch team glided into reception from a side door where they had been watching this little pantomime from the beginning.

"Gentlemen!" said the principal. "Gentlemen, what you have experienced for the last half hour or so is what your customers have to put up with every day of every week, every year. Let's go and see how we put that right, shall we?"

ABM won the business. That is the exemplar of the appropriate use of theater in a pitch.

> **Use theater only if it is *appropriate* for your client and *relevant* to your argument.**

When people ask me about using "theater" in pitches, that's the answer I always give. Using theatrical stunts can lift your pitch from the merely mundane to the magically compelling. Business folklore is littered with instances where pitching companies have used very extravagant techniques to demonstrate a point they wanted the client to understand, or to show how hungry they were to win the client's business. The reason these stunts go down in legend is that they *worked*. And the reason they worked is because they were appropriate to the client, to the situation the client was facing, and to the content of the presentation. Empty, vacuous stunts with no relevance will diminish your pitch rather than enhance it. **You can use theater to good effect only**

**if you have a deep appreciation of the client
organization and the critical issue it is facing.**

The middle

Attention will inevitably wane as you get into the body of
your presentation, so have something dramatic in the
middle section that reawakens the audience, smacks them
between the eyes, surprises and re-engages them. A clip of
film, a visual illustration, a section where the audience
participates. Get them to stand up, or walk about. Have a
break. If you have exciting ideas to show them, this is
where they appear.

In one company I worked for, two of the principals used
to sit next to each other and whisper frantically to each
other while one colleague was making the presentation.
This sounds rude and distracting, but they would start
writing and drawing and then, in the next pause in the
presentation, they would interrupt the agenda to explain
an idea they had just had. It wasn't really a new idea that
had just occurred. They'd rehearsed doing this to **make
the client believe that they had just witnessed the
birth of a great idea**. It visually reinforced the
impression that these people really did spark off one
another. And that is a very compelling impression to make.
A good impression helps to sell your ideas. (However,
beware of this particular technique. It works powerfully
when pitching to Expressives, but to Analyticals it could
look like you're making things up as you go along.
Remember, you have to know your audience.)

The ending

Make the end the climax. Don't go out with a whimper! *Don't* go out on: "Are there any questions?"

A friend of mine pitched for a national newspaper account. The newspaper had been losing readers to its rivals for over a decade. It needed to take drastic action to win readers back. In order to get the clients to understand that they really needed to do things differently, and to make them feel positive about doing so, my friend showed them a film clip from the Hollywood blockbuster *Apollo 13*. The film tells the story of how NASA's and the astronauts' teamwork and resourcefulness brought a stranded space crew safely back home. The clip my friend showed depicted the pilot of the damaged spacecraft firing the retro rockets in order to correct the angle at which their craft would re-enter the earth's atmosphere. Doing this was necessary but *highly* dangerous. If the rockets were on for too little time or for too long, the spacecraft would either burn up on re-entry or ricochet off the earth's outer atmosphere. The point of showing the clip was to demonstrate to the client that **taking radical action at the correct time can deliver transformational results**. If it could save lives it could save their newspaper.

Imagine you're the client. The pitch team plays this highly emotive film clip as the ending to their pitch. How does it make you feel? Emboldened? Excited? Challenged? Heroic? You bet. My friend walked out of the room with the business. Now *that's* an ending.

9 Smile

As a human being, you are unique on planet earth—
you can smile. No other creature can do this. Smiling is
allowed in business and is actually quite endearing to
other human beings. But you will only be able to smile if
you are relaxed (otherwise it will look like a rictus grin)
and you will only be relaxed if you have rehearsed. You
can also use humor. (Humor, in a pitch, when everything
is so serious? Surely not.) Humor shows the client team
that you're human, regular, down
to earth, that you have humility
and that you are more than just a
job function. Let your personality
out for the day!

> Give the client a bit of *you*.

10 Careless talk costs lives

Be paranoid about controlling the environment. One
world-famous company was pitching for a very large
telecoms client. At the end of the presentation the clients
asked if the pitching team would mind leaving the room
so they could discuss what had just been presented.
Once the pitching team had left the room, the clients got
up and strolled around the table discussing their views.
One client glimpsed some words scrawled on one of the
pitching team's notepads: "Who's the b*****d in the
glasses? He looks like trouble." After reading that, the
guy in the glasses *was* trouble. The pitching team had
indiscreetly written down a personal comment and it
cost them the business.

Confidentiality: be careful what you write down. Be careful what you leave lying around.

A company I once worked for pitched for, and won, a famous airline account. Immediately after they had made the pitch, the team collected up all their creative work (which was on big squares of cardboard) and stored it in the corner of their team leader's office. Next morning when they came in to work, they found a little colony of homeless people camped outside their front door, their new "homes" constructed from the presentation boards shown to the airline the day before. The office cleaners had thought the stack of cardboard was rubbish and had put it outside in the street for collection. The company's entire strategy was on the street for all to see.

Keep important work under lock and key!

Chapter 16
Unstoppable momentum

The client is highly anxious. After weeks of having handed over the responsibility for solving their problem to you, they now have to make a decision. The right decision. Careers ride on this decision. **The Golden Rule is: KEEP GOING!**

You must assume that it is a hung jury, that there is a split vote. The period after the pitch is when you must step up the momentum for the client jury to choose you. To give you, not the other guy, the benefit of the doubt. So you need any excuse to keep the initiative going, to display your absolute rightness for this job. The question is, how do you do this?

1 Detailed answers to questions

In the pitch they probably asked you some questions. You will have given them some answers there and then, but going back to your office affords you the chance to develop more detailed and better answers. Turn these answers into a mini document and send them within 12 hours of presenting.

2 Summarize why they should choose you.

3 Activate your "mole"

Remember the client's personal assistant who you've been befriending over the last three weeks? Call. Is there anything else that the clients need? What mood were they in when they returned from your presentation? Play the big-eyed puppy dog! Ask for some sort of reassurance that they didn't think you were all mad! Make that person laugh and they might just let you know something you can act on. All intelligence is useful at this stage.

4 Generate work

… and more work. And more work. Demonstrate to them that you have ideas that just keep coming. Energy (provided it is relevant) is very persuasive.

5 Be helpful

6 Never, never, never, never give up

It ain't over till it's over. The head of one famous advertising agency got a call saying they had come a close second. He asked the client why, and found out that the client had seen another creative solution they felt was spot on. He pressed the client (they had built a very strong relationship over the previous few weeks) and found out the gist of the idea.

"Damn!" exclaimed the agency head. "We had an idea along those lines and we decided not to present it only yesterday. Tell you what, are you around tomorrow morning?" (It was 5:00 pm.) "Why don't I come over and show it to you? There's no harm in seeing it." The client agreed.

The agency had no such angle. They worked all night, from scratch, to produce a new campaign. They just wouldn't say die. They went to the client's offices, presented the work and used the face-to-face time to convince the client that they were the right choice.

Is that cheating? Is that clever? Is that persistence? Wrong questions. Did it win? **Yes.**

Chapter 17
Feedback

Demand feedback, whether you win or lose.

If you win, ask the client in to help you celebrate and ask them if they'll be interviewed the following week by someone impartial at your company on what worked in the pitch and anything that could have been better.

If you lose, take the news graciously (**never make enemies**). Remember, the client has to make four or five of these calls to give bad news to very disappointed people. Don't make it any harder for them than it already is—they'll never forget it if you do. Ask if you can fix a de-brief for four weeks' time to come and ask them what went wrong. If you ask for feedback straight away, they'll just be nice to you, which is useless. In four weeks' time, 1) they will be honest and objective in their criticism and 2) the first cracks in their new relationship may have begun to show as the client realizes that what was promised by the winning company and what can actually be delivered are not necessarily the same. This gives you a second bite of the cherry. (This has worked for me twice in 500 pitches, but both times the prize was worth over a million euros.)

Never lose an opportunity to learn.

Here are some of the questions you will need to have answered in the course of your **Pitch Post-Mortem**:

> What did you think of our key people?

> What was the team chemistry like, both between our team and with your team?

> What should we do better?

> What did we do that we shouldn't do?

> What should we do that we didn't do?

> How did our pitch compare with our competitors'?

> How did we come over during the process and in the presentation?

> What other observations would you make?

PART 3

Special skills

Chapter 18
A world of difference—pitching internationally

We each start from a different perspective.

We all think we know what the world looks like; we're all familiar with the map of the world. Well, we're all familiar with *our* map of the world. But depending on where you are in the world, the map looks different. Why? Because it's the same world seen from a different perspective. A map of the world hung on a New York office wall has the Americas dead center in the middle of the map, with Europe off to the right-hand side and Australasia to the left-hand side. In Paris, Europe is front and center in the picture with the Americas off to the left and Asia off to the right. With such fundamentally different views of the world, pitching in foreign cultures can be fraught with problems. This chapter is designed to help you **avoid treading on cultural landmines**.

There are two sides to international pitching. The first is pitching **to** people from different cultures. The second is pitching **with** people from different cultures. Increasingly, we have to pitch for clients who are part of multinational organizations and whose pitch panels are made up of people from different nationalities or cultures. And in a global economy more and more business is pitched for non-domestic clients. In short, we have all to become

www.encompass-graphics.co.uk

more aware of the habits, customs, and behaviors of people from other cultures. Just by being aware of appropriate ways to behave or what to expect from different cultures in meetings can make the difference between winning and losing.

Pitching to people from different cultures

The International Olympic Committee (IOC) has two official languages: French and English. When Britain's prime minister, Tony Blair, made his part of the presentation to the IOC in Singapore on behalf of London's bid to host the 2012 Olympics, it cannot have helped but impress the members of the committee that he made his speech half in English and half in French. Behaving internationally rather than parochially goes a long way to delivering victory in international pitching. Show willing and you're halfway to victory.

Make a little go a long way. You may not have a native's command of nine different languages, but you can try to master a few basics in order to show a lack of arrogance or cultural ignorance. And how you behave says as much about you as what you say.

The basic tenet of successful international pitching is to walk a kilometer in the other person's shoes. **Put yourself in their position.** If you're from Detroit and you're pitching in Madrid, don't invite the clients out for dinner at six in the evening, like you would at home. They don't even think of going to a restaurant before 9:30 pm. And don't talk about business the moment you've sat down. Take your time, socialize, make small talk. You might drop business into the conversation over coffee, casually. Otherwise you're just being pushy and rude. Remember that Spain is a fiercely proud wine-producing country, so if you eat, you drink wine, not mineral water. Even at lunchtime.

I've seen a New Yorker, the president of a multinational company, incur the animosity of his entire audience with one opening remark. In his first sentence he referred to Labor Day, the vacation weekend that in his home country marks the official end to summer. With that one reference he signaled a total lack of empathy with his exclusively European audience. He hadn't been culturally attuned enough to recognize that no one in his audience cared about Labor Day. In his presentation, he showed a totally US-centric attitude to business and to the world. All his references were American. He showed, in short, that he didn't care enough to bother to moderate his language and his references to make them relevant to his audience. And they judged him for it.

So much of pitching success is about paying attention to the little things. The things you might not ordinarily notice. When they are done right, they go un-remarked. But when they go wrong they scream "WRONG!"

A run around the world: cultural landmines to watch out for

Remember, different cultures have different views on the world. Some cultures like things to be simple and uncomplicated; others like complexity and see it as evidence of a well-thought-through argument. America tends to look to the future and be optimistic; "old" Europe is often accused of looking to the past and being pessimistic. Some cultures are very black and white and use language and argument to clarify; others are much grayer in their world outlook, more relativist, less absolute—to the uninitiated, their use of language may seem to hide and obfuscate. Anglo-Saxons tend to prize individualism and argument; the Japanese are more collectivist and consensual.

Whatever you are pitching for, and wherever you are doing it, take the time and make the effort to understand their needs better than your competitor—and **demonstrate you've taken the time and made the effort**.

It is difficult to generalize about

> **Take the time and make the effort to understand cultural differences.**

cultural nuances. However, below are some brief pointers that might stop you and your team trampling all over local sensitivities. Westerners worry about pitching in two regions more than any others: the Middle East and Asia. Here is a quick guide to what to watch out for if you are making a pitch in those regions.

Asia

There are vast differences between the different countries of Asia. The most I can do is give you a flavor of some obvious differences in business etiquette in each of the major markets within the area: Japan, China, Hong Kong, Singapore, Thailand, Korea, and Australia.

Japan

> Never ever forget business cards. In Asia you will need one for every single person you meet. Running out of business cards reflects badly on your organizational skills.

> The giving and receiving of business cards is a ritual of great importance. If possible, cards should be in both English and Japanese. You should present your business card with both hands, holding the card at each corner, with the type facing toward the recipient (and with the Japanese language side up!).

> The way in which you receive a business card is also very important. You should accept a card with both hands and study it. Spending an exaggerated amount of time doing this will be seen as respectful. Do not put the card in your pocket. It should stay on the meeting table in front of you for the duration of the meeting and then be packed away neatly at the end, not stuffed into the nearest pocket and never left on the table.

> Don't give too much information away in a meeting. The decision maker will probably be in the room, but it is likely that no decision will be made in the meeting.

> The person who speaks to you most in the meeting will usually *not* be the most senior person in the room.

> Avoid lots of eye contact. This will be seen as confrontational and will make your host feel nervous and threatened. Take a more humble approach.

> The most senior person may well sit in the back and have an interpreter sitting next to them if you are presenting in English. This person may well close their eyes as you are presenting. They have not gone to sleep (you hope), they are just focusing on what the interpreter is saying. They are blocking out the charts and your voice to understand better what you are saying.

> When you finish your presentation, there may be a silence that stretches for minutes before anyone says anything. Don't jump in and try to fill the silence as you would in a pitch to a Western audience. This is considered ill-mannered. Don't interpret silence as lack of understanding or disapproval. Silence really is golden—it is the Japanese way of considering what has been said.

> The rules of "Face": If you ask a direct question and they don't know the answer, they'll reply along the lines of: "That's a difficult question" or "There's much that needs to be considered." Don't push them into a position where they have to say, "I don't know." If you do, you've embarrassed them in front of their peers and in front of your team and they may *never* work with you again. The Japanese must be allowed to keep face. They don't like saying they don't know, and they don't like having to say no.

> Listen for clues in the language being used. "That's not an avenue we can go down," or "That will be difficult," both mean "No."

> Business attire: in every circumstance you must wear formal business attire. If the client invites you for a second meeting and stipulates "No tie required," this is an invitation to wear business casual dress. Just as many American or European companies have Dress Down Friday, so some Japanese companies have no-tie days. But you must wait to be invited to wear no tie.

China

> Meeting etiquette is generally similar to Japan (including the business card ritual). However, it is much more likely that the senior decision maker will engage with you more than the rest of the client's team.

> Any 'green' Westerner will probably walk away thinking they've just had the best pitch of their career. The Chinese really engage with you—they ask loads of questions, they drill down into the detail of what you are saying, they say yes a lot (because they won't say no). The Chinese are brilliant at extracting information and see no problem in sharing that information with other colleagues and potential business partners. Just be wary of how much information or intellectual property you divulge. Let them know you know more, but that's what they will be buying.

> Be aware of different standards of living: if you say you drive to work in an Audi and own your own house it will sound to the average Chinese client like someone telling you they fly to work in a Learjet and own their own island just off the Côte d'Azur. In China very few people can afford to own a house.

> Don't be overfamiliar.

Hong Kong, Singapore, Thailand

> Much more Westernized than Japan and China in the style of meetings.
> Your attire may need to be formal or casual, depending on the company.
> Think of a mixture between London and Los Angeles!

Korea

> More Westernized than China and Japan.
> Never, ever, fill your own glass, either in a meeting or at dinner. Always fill your host's glass.
> The rules of "Face" apply here as in Japan.

Australia

> Think California rather than New York. Don't be pompous or a stuffed shirt.

A faux pas to avoid in Asia. *Never* stick your chopsticks into the rice in your rice bowl. This resembles incense sticks stuck into rice, which is a form of offering at funerals and therefore a symbol of death. It would be looked on very poorly by your hosts. Use the rests provided for your chopsticks when not in use.

If all else fails, follow the lead of your hosts.

Arab cultures

There is a story about an American brand of washing powder that launched in the Arab market. To demonstrate the effectiveness of the detergent, the brand team always showed two pictures of a white shirt—one crumpled and dirty, before it was washed, and one after it had been washed in their detergent. The dirty shirt was on the left of the poster, and the spotless washed shirt was on the right. For a Western audience, used to reading left to right, this was crystal-clear communication: a simple "Before and After" product demonstration to show how this brand of washing powder removed stains and left your white clothes dazzlingly clean.

But no one thought how such a product demonstration might be interpreted in a culture that reads right to left.

So when the posters went up all over the Arab cities where the detergent was launched, the population read the poster to mean that it turned clean clothes into a dirty, crumpled mess. Who, in their right mind, would want a product that made clean clothes filthy?

Here are some quick examples of how to signal you aren't an insensitive cultural Philistine.

> Start by greeting your clients in their own language to break the ice: "Salamu Alaikum" (Peace be upon you).

> Take time to chat with the clients and have Arabic coffee or tea with them. (Alcohol is forbidden to Moslems.)

> During Ramadan don't ask for a drink, even water, until after sundown. (Show them you appreciate their religious obligations.)

> Men should not shake a woman's hand *unless* she extends her hand first.

> Devout Moslem men will not shake a woman's hand.

> Introduce the team and have a native speaker in the meeting with you, on your team.

> Be very clear about costs (no hidden charges). Specify what is and what is not included.

> Show them you understand the limitations or rules of your discipline in their region. If there are certain cultural impediments to operating in the same way as you would in the West or elsewhere, let them know that you know this.

Meetings will take longer than planned. This is the norm in the Middle East.

Europe

For non-Europeans pitching in European countries, generally speaking there are fewer cultural landmines but watch out for local differences or sensitivities. German-speaking countries tend to be more formal, more rigid, more "Analytical," and hierarchy can be very important. Formal business attire and being very respectful to senior people are important. You must address senior people by their full titles, for example "Herr Doktor Brecht" rather than just "Doktor Brecht." Latin cultures can also be a little protocol led; proud people don't like being made fun of. And Scandinavians are ruthlessly straight talking and brutally honest; they will tell you exactly what they think of your presentation.

Pitching with people from different cultures

You have been asked to head an international team from your company—spanning five regional offices—to pitch for a massive multinational account worth millions. Do you react:

YIPPEE!!!!!

Your first reaction could well be unfettered enthusiasm for the task ahead. But most people's experience of working with their colleagues from overseas—many of whom they have probably never met—is more like:

Yippee.

Pitching is hard enough when you're trying to run it from one office, for one client, with a team of people who speak the same language, and who work in the same building. It is a million times more fraught when run over multiple markets, across myriad time zones, with teams of people with different agendas, profit-and-loss responsibilities, and cultural mores.

The styles of pitch are also different. French pitches can be long, wordy, intellectual debates intended to construct a unifying, theoretical, rationalist Grand Design out of the component parts of the argument. Anglo-Saxon pitches are reductionist, short, and pithy, boiling everything down to one simple core point, with lots of evidence grounded in reality. No wonder the French and the London offices of the same company can seem to the prospective client to be entirely separate animals.

When pitching in a team made up of people from different nationalities, it is beneficial to understand the behavior that will get your team acting as one, rather than as a loose federation of individuals whose respective home countries may have been at loggerheads for centuries. **International pitching means more than having someone show up for your team in order to read the PowerPoint slides in a foreign accent.**

You can get a long way to achieving international-pitch Nirvana by remembering a few, very fundamental principles.

1 **We respond quicker and better for people we know.** Even if it is the least you do, make sure your pitching specialists or new business directors sit down to break bread with each other regularly. The simple act of spending an evening talking—about anything but business—over a few drinks will multiply your inter-office cooperation quotient by a thousand. This is very handy when you pick up the phone and need information and help at very short notice. Think that's obvious? When was the last time you had a drink or dinner with your counterpart in Frankfurt, Bangkok, Adelaide, or Amsterdam? Why should they move Heaven and Earth for you?

2 **Don't be arrogant.** Speaking English with an unusual accent doesn't mean you're any less intelligent.

3 **Show respect.** Country size does not equal office size.

4 **Appoint a benign dictator who is in overall charge of the pitch effort.** This person must be capable of differentiating between bullshit and brilliance in 37 different languages.

5 **Get the most senior management to buy in immediately**, at each office within your network, in order to mobilize the necessary resources early and effectively.

6 **Design and distribute simple templates** so you can streamline the way information is fed in to the central office team. Standardize how information or content is to be reported. Make it easy for all offices to deliver what is needed efficiently.

7 **Allocate reasonable budgets** to make participation affordable and practical.

8 **Be crystal-clear about roles** and who is expected to do what and with whom.

9 **Be ruthless with everyone's diary**—especially the top people. They must be flown in 36 to 48 hours before the pitch so they can rehearse together and get the chemistry going.

10 **Give responsible feedback** on the pitch during and after it. Often, once the pitch is made, that's the last your Milan office hears about it until they discover eight months later that you won it.

11 **Thank everyone.**

Chapter 19
Pitching to government

Pitching to national government departments takes pitching on to a whole new level. The stakes are always high and can make the reputation of the victorious team.

So how do you secure such prestigious business?

It has always been my belief that the team who can make a client's pitch panel feel that they are doing something earth-shatteringly important, the business equivalent of sending a man to the moon, will win. If this is true for clients who make biscuits, or cars, or who help people buy their homes, then it is true one thousandfold for those who are building the transport infrastructure for a whole country, or trying to educate the population to eat more healthily. The one absolutely essential requirement for winning massive engineering—or social engineering—projects is to share the messianic zeal their creators have for them.

All the **rules** we've gone through to date are still valid, with bells on. But some of the **weapons and tricks** available to the pitching team in private enterprise are eliminated (on paper at least) when you're pitching to government.

The thing about government pitches is to remember that **the whole process has to be seen to be unimpeachably fair**. **Transparent. Objective.** It is the role of the process to eliminate, as much as is humanly possible, the emotion, prejudice, and relationship

distractions that could cloud the panel's judgment.
To ensure tax payers' money is being spent efficiently,
government pitches are rigorously modulated, with rules
of engagement written down, and the overall process
policed rigorously under the gimlet eyes of purchasing
specialists. A government official told me:

> [We] will employ the company that answers the brief
> the best. All the schmoozing, tactics, stunts, etc. don't
> work. We develop a marking system based on the
> project objectives and a selection panel would mark
> each pitch on how well they have aligned their proposal.
> A scoring matrix would usually be used to facilitate the
> process and the one that achieved the highest rating
> would be awarded the business.

Just as an aside, do you think the person who said this is
an Expressive, an Amiable, a Driver, or an Analytical (see
chapter 11)? Look at the type of words used as well as
what is being said. Words like *system*, *aligned*, *process*,
matrix, *rating* spell **ANALYTICAL** in capital letters.
Gives you a great clue as to how to operate with this
person to maximum effect.

Of course, outstanding pitch practitioners will *always* find
a way to tip the playing field in their favor, even when
pitch protocols exist in written and supposedly inflexible
form. That's the game.

The process

Most contracts funded out of the public purse, or that
involve government interests, or that are operated by
publicly accountable bodies, will go through several

formal stages. Such contracts must be seen to be open to all qualified contenders, and so begin with a formal notice in the various relevant media or journals inviting applications to tender. Many publicly funded organizations will operate a list of pre-approved and vetted suppliers of the relevant skills required, and so the vital thing for any professional services company hoping to contend for such contracts is to get on this official list. Normally this is a combination of base criteria (financial stability, skill base, client list, accreditation to the professional body) and qualitative judgments, for example about the reputation of the company and its staff. It is important to remember that commissioning bodies in the public sector are under the most severe scrutiny. They must, therefore, ensure that those companies with which they do business are either demonstrably safe choices (along the lines of the adage "No one ever got fired for hiring IBM"), or at the very leading edge of their specialist field.

The criteria

The tendering stage (Request for Information: RFI) always produces multiple applications. Government business is attractive—even if the commercial terms are not always so—because of its profile and because it is usually stimulating and exciting. Consequently, the poor benighted souls whose job it is to screen the tidal wave of initial applications, are actively looking for excuses to *exclude* rather than include your company on the long list of suppliers who will go through to the next stage. Don't give them any avoidable reasons to bin your submission—

no spelling mistakes! (I once saw a submission that went with a covering letter with three spelling mistakes in it, plus the client's name was incorrectly spelled. This was from a company that was re-tendering to keep the business that they had had for seven years.)

Answer all the questions.

In addition, they will be looking for evidence of your company's:

> previous experience with the department
> relevant experience on the issue or subject of the project
> special insight or expertise
> understanding of governmental or public-sector modus operandi
> track record on delivery
> commitment to targets and evaluation
> market reputation
> management team's strength and profile
> size, resource, and stability.

Deliver your submission three days before the deadline.

Deliver your submission three days before the deadline. Ninety-five percent of respondents will submit their document three hours before the deadline. (Government departments notice things like this.) Just doing this alone will make you stand out as different and will signal that you are taking it very seriously. Get the easy bits right.

The governmental client

Unlike private-sector pitches, there will often be multiple constituencies involved with the decision. Even if, in reality, only one person will make the ultimate decision on which supplier to appoint on a particular project, many voices need to be seen to have had their say. It's just the system of checks and balances that prevents personal agendas holding sway. So the chances are that lots of people will attend your pitch. There tends to be a lot of consultation within government, which means lots of different people and groups will have an input. As the pitcher, it is important you understand all the influencer groups and address their specific issues. Additionally, you will need to talk with "naive intelligence" outside the department about the issues under consideration: lobbyists, journalists, social researchers, the voluntary sector, unions, Citizens Advice Bureaux—anyone who can help you get the 360-degree perspective, not just the official one.

Despite all these contributing voices, it is vital you identify the key decision maker. Remember that there are at least two thick layers to get through in government. First, the civil servants, then the Ministers. (They are not always in agreement!) For example, in pitches for communications projects within the British government, the policy official is often the key decision maker, followed by the Whitehall communications mandarin and then the specialist advisers—in this instance the Central Office of Information (COI). When they are completely happy, the Minister will be involved. Civil servants seek to have information ready to answer any challenges and questions from senior colleagues or Ministers. So all your recommendations must be accompanied by rationales that can be used "upstairs."

You must research the Minister who has ultimately to approve the work. Do his political and personal agendas coincide with the brief you have? What vision has he personally expressed for the policy? What does this tell you about the tone of your pitch, the degree of drama, the social context of the announcement? Look for hidden agendas. You must understand the political requirement, the political dimension—what's all this really about?

Overall, there are some golden rules to remember when pitching for government business.

1 **There is a "mafia of voices"**—from the most junior official right up to the Secretary of State, word will get around if you are seen as a good lot. This is a close-knit community. Don't rely on one or two close contacts. You will need friends all along the way.

2 **Junior officials don't like being treated as unimportant** and they will look for any opportunity to bring about your downfall if you treat them badly. Treat all of them with respect.

3 **Put your most senior people on the team**, and make them go to all the meetings—even with junior officials.

4 **Government officials admire longevity of service and consistency of team.** Don't constantly shift people around your team. Keep a few, good, senior people with staying power.

5 Have a *real* understanding of the subject— whether it's pensions or tax credits, health policy or diversity. You really need to know the subject matter. You cannot bluff it—the policy official will spot you a mile off. (Get to know the policy official.)

6 Small teams, small meetings—if at all possible.

7 The Secretary of State

> All Secretaries of State and Ministers are **experts** (even if you don't think they are).

> All Secretaries of State and Ministers are **bullies**. They will test you to see if you have conviction in what you are recommending. They do this with their own staff, so they'll definitely do it with you. Whatever you do, don't give in. Once you've conceded ground today, you will not regain it tomorrow.

> For a pitch to the Secretary of State you'll be given half an hour. You will get only **ten minutes**— Secretaries of State always run late. Hone your pitch into five minutes.

> When you are presenting to the Secretary of State **you're on your own**. Don't look for support. It won't arrive.

> **Beware of last-minute ministerial intervention.** Ministers are dealing with a huge portfolio of issues so they are not always focused on your issue early on. When they do focus, they will be ruthless and they will not care about your deadlines.

> To win business with government you need to build an **aura of trust** around you and your team. Never, ever, be late. Never, ever, let them down. Never, ever,

fail to deliver on the date promised. You'll never work for them again (remember the "mafia of voices").

The need to demonstrate effect

Policy officials and specialist advisers are the real clients and are *very* expert in their field. They operate under massive time pressure and in an extremely volatile environment. The importance of expenditure control and the source of the money they spend (tax payers) means they are visibly accountable. You must speak in the language of accountability: cost–benefit analysis, return on investment (ROI), evaluation, and measurement. Living under the shadow of potentially hostile attack from pressure groups or the media, governmental clients will be unlikely to award business on the basis of your faith in what you might, or should, be able to deliver. Things that cannot be measured don't tend to be valued. Shock tactics or wacky solutions are most unlikely to appeal—these people are not inclined to "take a flyer."

Equally, you may need to convince the policy officials of the importance of your expertise to the issue. Don't assume it is accepted or taken as read. Get as many face-to-face meetings as you can, and if they offer any meetings, take them! Getting access to these people is rare.

Government business is always important and usually fascinating. It's worth the investment to get to grips with the peculiarities of how it works in order to win it. It may not pay the bills as well as other sectors, but that's more than compensated for with the profile it can bring to your company.

Chapter 20
Writing compelling tender documents

A tender, or a Request for Information (RFI), is like a first date. All your senses, and those of your potential partner, are on red alert. The person looking at the tender document is trying to sniff out your faults, look for mistakes, listen out for inconsistencies, feel for your weaknesses and get an overall taste of what you will be like. Your submission needs to look the part, be on its best behavior, pay care and attention, so the reader will get an immediate sense of all your good qualities.

Your tender document must delight and surprise. If you only tick all the boxes you will not differentiate yourself against the competition. You need to start adding considerable value even at this stage. Sectionalize your submission to add qualitative elements as well as the quantitative information that has been asked for. Put a little soul into your document. If you look at the anatomy of a great tender, it goes well beyond the brief. It covers all the basics but also gives a viewpoint on:

> the challenge (of the project)

> staffing (appropriate people and the values of the team)

> resources that the tendering company can draw upon and which are unique

> measuring effect (special techniques, track record, or just a willingness to be accountable)

> the service the client can expect (processes, techniques, reporting)
> network affiliations and specialist expertise
> quality assurance (systems, sign-offs, confidentiality, compliance)
> remuneration.

In other words, to stand out you will have to go WAY BEYOND what is asked for or expected. I've seen lots of examples of what happens when you don't apply imagination and flair but simply churn the things out like painting by numbers:

Your response was comprehensive, in-depth, detailed and absolutely full of relevant experience—but it had no surprises. The client was looking to be excited and enthused. You failed to provide a vehicle to convey your enthusiasm through the submission.

[De-brief to direct marketing agency]

Clients, especially governmental clients, want to learn something new, even at this early stage of the process. And this is where the Super-Pitcher will recognize an opportunity to get a head start on the competition, to turn a passive process into an active one where you can influence the criteria on which the submissions are judged. Super-Pitchers will help the reader of a tender by sharing their experience with him. You can add considerable value by itemizing the key questions which, in your company's experience, are helpful in evaluating submissions or selecting the appropriate supplier. There's a chance that your criteria might make it on to the final list used by the client. And those criteria will probably be qualities your company has in abundance.

Tender documents: dos and don'ts

DO:

1 Make a call

> Get talking, discuss the request.
> What are they really looking for?
> What are the evaluation criteria?

Tender-commissioning departments usually like to stay aloof and tight-lipped, but you can at least establish contact and try to elicit useful information in order to deliver a more relevant tender.

2 Provide great navigation

> Sectionalize.
> Provide a Contents page.
> Number each page.
> Put key points in the margin.
> Use sub-headings and highlights.
> Use diagrams to illustrate your systematic processes and development tools.

3 Keep an armory of the information you will always need, and keep it up to date:

> Report and accounts.
> Number of staff by discipline area.
> Résumés of staff's experience, expertise, professional body memberships.
> Published articles written by your company's staff.
> Trade press/media commentary on your company.

> Client testimonials.

> Awards.

4 **Package your tender.** Make it memorable.
I remember one submission that arrived packaged in a whiskey crate (this was relevant to the brief).

5 **KISS—Keep It Simple, Stupid.** If you must use technical jargon, have the good sense and good manners to explain what it means. Otherwise, avoid long, complicated, multi-clausal sentences that use five words to do a job one word could do better. Don't overcomplicate things in the mistaken belief that this makes them sound more profound.

6 **Differentiate your methodology.** Show the benefit of your way of doing things. The only real benefit is the better results it produces for your clients. Don't get lost in the detail of how you do stuff; do emphasize what it means to the client.

7 **Be a straight shooter.** Find a way to admit a fault or mistake and what you did as a result, or to put into context your contribution to the overall success of a project. Don't make incredible claims.

8 **Have a theme** running through your whole submission—a look, a feel, a style, a thread of plot to help you focus and draw out the key points.

9 **Write a management summary** and a covering letter that demonstrates your extra value to, and motivation for, this project.

10 **Triple proofread.** Read the document at least three times, preferably with at least 24 hours between each read.

DON'T:

1 **Ignore it** until it's urgent.

2 **Get people's job titles and names wrong.**

3 **Strike a note of false chumminess.**

4 **Write the tender by rote.** Avoid the "canned" response or the temptation to do a stick-and-paste job from five previous tender documents.

5 **Be long-winded.**

6 **Lack style or personality.**

7 **Rush your fee quotation**—you'll live to regret it.

Remember: the devil is in the detail.

Bear in mind the target audience for the tender submission. Often tender submissions are divided among several different reader groups who will evaluate the documents from different specialist perspectives. In terms of the general level of presentation for tender documents, the bar has been raised continually and remorselessly over the last few years. One submission among potentially hundreds needs to stand out against the competition. It needs to read well, easily, succinctly, and—sometimes—entertainingly. It must be easy to navigate and signpost the relevant information clearly. Don't make the mistake of producing these things by rote or on a simple template. If you do, you'll disappear. Tender documents require design and editing skills. You need to prepare them from the reader's perspective and with care and attention to detail.

PART 4
Getting it sorted

Chapter 21
Top tips

What should you do if you are asked to work on a pitch?

1 Accept … and accept enthusiastically. Why?

a) It is a sign that the company rates you.

b) It is a chance to be prominent, to shine.

c) It is an opportunity to work intensely with the very top management over a very concentrated period of time—you will learn a lot.

d) It is a novel experience away from the everyday routine of normal business.

e) It will sharpen your skills.

f) It gives you a chance to work on an interesting new market with, hopefully, interesting new clients on brilliant new work.

g) It might just be fun.

2 Acknowledge that you are in for some very hard work

a) You must still carry out your normal duties.

b) Pitching is unforgiving of lackluster effort or a *mañana* attitude.

c) You will need to work longer hours, be faster on your feet, and generally be extremely organized.

3 Acknowledge that you will need to make your pitch everybody else's main priority

Your colleagues are busy. You will need to persuade, cajole, push, and pull them through the next few weeks. Just as you cannot be sparing of your own effort, neither can they. You will not be popular ... you will need to energize and motivate exemplary performance from your entire team.

4 Clear the decks

a) Organize your diary.

b) Sacrifices may have to be made to your social/home life—they are only temporary but they will happen. Remember (as an old colleague of mine used to say):

> Your reward is in the car park.

5 What do you know, and need to know, about the potential client?

a) Sector? Audience? People? Reputation? Track record? Advisers? Is this a client you've worked with before? Is this an important win for you? What's their track record as a client and buyer of your services? Do we have a client conflict? Who do we know at their advisers?

b) Who is the decision maker? Who are the internal and external influencers on the decision? What are their buying habits and characteristics? What are the dynamics and politics between the client team? Are they experienced buyers of your services?

c) Why is there a pitch? What does the client want to buy? Is it a new project? Are they unhappy with the incumbent? (Why?) Are they trying to drive down price?

d) What will win you this pitch? Price? Technical competency? Systems and process? Sector expertise?

6 Good sources of information about the company

a) Their own literature:
> annual report
> sales brochures
> internet site
> company brochures

b) Experts:
> editors of trade journals
> journalists
> sales force
> retailers
> academics
> authors of books in this market
> ex-clients
> company staff
> client's suppliers (bankers, lawyers, public relations, design, sales promotion, media, advertising agencies)
> staff
> analysts' reports
> lobby groups
> blogs

c) "Factory" tour

d) Published data

e) Advertising

f) Research groups

Chapter 22
Checklists for winning

Playing at home list

1 Confirm, all in writing: venue, date, time, attendees (theirs and ours), their travel arrangements, duration of meeting

2 Reception briefed

3 Outside of building tidy
   > Lights working
   > Toilets tidy
   > Our company emailed and aware
   > Relevant trade journal on reception

4 Pitch team in the room, ready

5 Coffee, tea, soft drinks, biscuits, lunch, etc. (*Their* brands if relevant!)

6 Food arranged (special dietary requirements)

7 Parking spaces booked

8 Taxis booked

9 Pitching room:
   > What's on the walls
   > Props arranged
   > TV/sound clips cued up
   > Equipment/laptop functioning (*Their* brand of equipment if they make it!)
   > New batteries in slide console/remote
   > Technical backup arranged

> Agendas
> Name cards (spelled correctly)
> Presentation backup (documents, etc.) in case equipment fails
> Business cards
> Notices "Meeting in Progress"

Playing away list

Same as "at home," plus:

1 Recce the room before your presentation. Draw a plan of room detailing:
   > Power points
   > Position of table/door/windows
   > How to block out light if needed?
   > Where should clients sit for best views?

   Ascertain what equipment is available and if there is a technical expert on hand. Book him for the duration of your presentation, or line up technical support from your company. Ascertain if you can get into the room 15–30 minutes before the actual presentation in order to set up.

2 Line up equipment backup:
   > PowerPoint projector and screen
   > Extension leads
   > Plug fuses
   > DVD/video/monitor/CD, etc.

3 Confirm in writing to the client and whoever is in charge of the room (admin and technical) at the client company. Call 48 hours in advance of presentation to re-confirm equipment, etc.

4 Travel arrangements to be centrally coordinated by team's personal assistant. Ensure each team member is briefed personally about where, when, how, etc. and at final rehearsal re-confirm to the whole team.

Chapter 23
Client checklist—tick all their boxes

Client's criteria for pitch selection

1 Previous relevant experience in our sector/category
2 Track record with our organization
3 Special insight into issue/problem/audiences
4 Understanding of our operating environment
5 Ability to deliver solution
6 Reputation
7 Cost effectiveness—commitment to targets and evaluation
8 Strength of senior management
9 Company size and resources available
10 Financial stability
11 Recent new business performance
12 Position within their own sector
13 Reputation with intermediaries

14 Performance against industry benchmarks/surveys/league tables

15 Relevance of proposed solution

16 Creativity of proposed solution

17 Chemistry of pitching team

18 Culture of company

19 People and environmental policy

20 Clarity of thinking and reputation for delivery

Chapter 24
The greatest pitcher of all time

At the beginning of this book I said it was easier to come first than to come a close second. If you adopt all the techniques in this book, you will have more success—you will win more, and it will seem easy. **Victorious teams always have more energy left at the end of the race than losing teams.** Next time you watch the Oxford vs Cambridge Boat Race, look at the victors and how much energy they've got compared to the losers, who are collapsed on their oars.

But the truth is that, whatever the result, pitching, like any competitive endeavor, is hard work. If you've spent years chasing a goal or a client you want to work with, don't you owe it to yourself to take advantage of anything that will tilt the odds of winning in your favor?

Alexander the Great knew this. And Alexander was the greatest new-business pitcher of all time. By the age of 32 he had conquered the entire known world.

Alexander was entirely focused on winning. His genius lay in adopting the approach I have described in this book, implementing it relentlessly and, most crucially, tipping the playing field in his favor. He looked for competitive advantage in all his military campaigns. Depending on your point of view, he either innovated or cheated.

Corbis

When confronted with the famed puzzle of the Gordian knot, instead of trying to unravel the convoluted knot, he simply sliced through the ropes. When facing the Uxians, instead of engaging them in conventional battle, he marched his way over a mountain, at night, and massacred the enemy in their beds.

What's the point? Alexander had a goal. You have a goal. He chased that goal for ten years. You'll chase a new business prospect for years before you get the chance to pitch for it. When you do, remember Alexander—when you get the chance, do everything in your power to seize the prize. Don't play by everyone else's conventions. Make your own luck.

In the wee small hours, when you're tired and you want to go home, and the pitch you are working on is hard graft, make that extra effort, apply the disciplines of professional business development and, like Alexander, you will also

Weep, for there are no worlds left to conquer.

PART 5

Quick pitch "to do" lists

Total immersion, unstoppable energy, loads of enthusiasm, thousands of initiatives, intensive care, attention to detail, courtesy, fun & friendly

Table 1

The "At-a-glance pitch guide"

Organization	Preparation	The client	The competition
1 Internal > Core team > Allocate roles > Timing plan > Status reports > Daily meetings > 24-hour brainstorm > Information bible > Book rooms for meetings > Coordinate diaries > Brief secretaries > Write up meetings **2 External** > Client organogram > Contact tel nos/emails > Diary dates for weekly meetings > Diary dates to see: CEO/MD, financial director, etc. Sales staff Ops/technical Researchers "Factory" tour Legal staff PR dept/agency > Anyone who will attend the pitch > Social > Away day > Invite to research groups	**For initial meeting** > Team briefed? > Know: Market size? Trends? Stakeholders? Seasonality? Regionality? Factors influencing? Media usage? Seen website? Product positioning? Visited outlets? Visited stores where sold? Bought/used product? Done research groups? > List of questions to ask? > Point of view developed? > Relevant case studies? > What will they want to know about your company? > Take-aways: Facts & figures re: your company, bit of fun to show you're keen	**Pitch for people, not products!** > What do we know about the clients? > Search press articles > Intermediaries > Relevant contacts > Who will be at pitch? > Who is the real decision maker? **Remember: they are anxious** > Get to know them, like them, get them to like you > Make them feel they're in safe hands, e.g.: Operational guides Contact report meetings & phone conversations > Show them how you will run their business **Demonstrate commitment** Listen! Ask questions: > Why a pitch? > How do they like to work? > What practices make them furious? **Judging criteria** > What do they want to see on the day? > Any checklist of factors they will mark? > Try to influence those criteria	**Know the enemy** > Who are you up against? > Why has the client chosen each competing company? > Why chosen you? > What do they expect from you? > Is size a likely issue? > What is your positioning in this pitch relative to competition? > What are the other pitching companies likely to come up with? > How will they run their pitch? > Do any of the clients have personal relationships with staff at other pitching companies? > Emotionally, who does the client want to win?

Etiquette	The brief	Try harder	Work	Pitch
Every contact is an opportunity to impress	**Does client have clear view on:**	**Passion persuades**	**This pitch is the company's No.1 priority**	> When, where, who?

Etiquette

Every contact is an opportunity to impress

> How long have they got?
> Travel/parking organized?
> Reception briefed?
> Public areas tidy?
> Toilets tidy?
> Refreshments (special dietary requirements?)?
> Seating plan?
> Agenda?
> Appropriate room for occasion/mood?
> Equipment tested?
> VT/audio cued?
> Props ordered?
> Wall decoration?
> Role for all team?
> Offer to show around your company
> Their energy level (where are you in their schedule?)

Considerations for pitching at client's office

> Recce room/site
> Draw room plan
> Ask for 30 mins to set up
> Take spare equipment
> Test sound levels
> Refreshments?
> Be early!
> What equipment have they got?
> What equipment do you need?

The brief

Does client have clear view on:

> What the solution is meant to achieve?
> What they expect from you?
> How target audience sees client now?
> How you want target audience to see brand in the future?
> Budget?
> Timings?
> Restrictions & Mandatories

Does client have prejudices?

> Sort of work they have bought?
> Have they told you the ideal solution?
> What are the client's real concerns?

Try harder

Passion persuades

> Get to see as many people in as many departments at client as you can
> Interview their trade customers
> Interview their customers (invite client to watch research groups)
> Accompanied shopping visits
> Interview trade journalists
> Interview/read experts
> Interview/show ideas to journalists/ editors of relevant consumer publications
> Interview trade bodies/ associations
> Pose as student and interview client's competitors

Go the extra mile

> Give them an analysis of their competitors
> Write and thank everyone who has given time to help/answer questions
> Send them press cuttings of interesting articles
> Attend their trade shows (at least know what & when they are)

Work

This pitch is the company's No.1 priority

> Brief in an inspiring way
> Fight for the best/most appropriate team
> Drop everything when the teams want your help/need to speak to you: there isn't much time
> Be aware of legal issues for this market
> Line up parties for quick approvals
> What do you need to sell the work (props)?
> Client meet team?
> Copies of work for document

Pitch

> When, where, who?
> Charts
> Edit, edit, edit
> Do you need to present your company's credentials?
> Rehearse, be ruthless on logic, handovers, style
> What do you want them to remember?
> Tone?
> What are they being asked to buy? Is it clear & well defined?
> Timing: clock in room/time master
> Balance
> Spelling & typing errors
> Listen & watch
> Is your introduction gripping?
> Is your ending compelling?
> Prepare written answers to questions
> Details:
  Timing plan
  Costings
  Evaluation
  Remuneration
  Document/take-away
> Have you visited presentation room at client? Room dressed?
> Backup technical staff lined up?
> Transport arrangements
> Display boards
> Client's products on display?
> Food & drinks?
> Client's itinerary

Table 2

Example of a week-by-week pitch action plan

Item	Before	Week 1
1 Administration	Secretarial resource. Briefing meeting. Assemble team and circulate brief: > allocate roles & workload > book rooms for internal meetings > source information pack > source client's competitors' intelligence > order trade/professional magazines > compile dossier on client of all info gleaned	Daily team meetings. Book rooms for client meetings. Organogram of clients. Establish rules of contact. Ask client for last presentation slot at the pitch.
2 Client	Press cuttings on key personnel. Anyone known to you or colleagues elsewhere. Call & ask what they need to see/want to discuss. Do homework on the client team.	Set up weekly/bi-weekly meetings. Set up social with clients. Diary clients for research groups. Agree pitch success/ judging criteria. Brainstorm with your company's top talent.
3 Strategy	Read trade mags/interviews. Consumer groups/panels. Annual report. Speak to PR department at client.	Write draft brief. Meet with sales force, PR, academic experts. Competitive analysis. Audit client's research. Conduct research groups. Number crunching (business, target audience).
4 Presentation	For initial meeting: > attendees > case studies > demonstration of effort and knowledge > have a viewpoint about their situation	Location of pitch: room plan. Equipment booking. Secretarial support, diary rehearsals.

Week 2	Week 3	Week 4	Week 5 Post-pitch
Daily team meetings. Work up logistics presentation of how you will run the client's business at your company. Set up systems, extranet/intranet, etc.	Daily team meetings. Write to client to confirm all arrangements for the pitch day. Brief in any production jobs, e.g. place cards, props, etc.	Daily team meetings. Brief your team on all pitch arrangements. Walk through the timetable of the pitch day. Put your company on alert if client is visiting your offices.	Ensure team is de-briefed immediately after the pitch. Respond to questions asked by clients in written form with detailed answers. Summarize why they should appoint you. Keep going!
Client meeting(s) > take through logistics of how you'll work with them. Your top management interview their top management. Brainstorm with client.	Client meeting(s). Pre-test strategies/ concepts with core client team.	Client meeting(s). Rev up the client team with every contact you have with them. Impress them with your attention to detail & conviction.	Agree timetable for when client will respond to your pitch. Ask if they need anything else. Keep working! Find tactical ways to remain engaged.
Focus on getting the answer. Torture-test your hypotheses. Re-read the brief. Check if you've covered all the areas.	Trade customers, journalist. Research your solutions. Draft the management summary. Finalize recommendations.	Polish your strategic recommendation.	Gauge reaction to your proposal. Look for ways to reinforce its rightness for the client's situation . . . or finesse it in light of client comments made at pitch.
Write/logic flow of presentation. Start writing the presentation.	First run-through of presentation. Second run-through of presentation. Rehearsal 1. Focus on bringing the recommendation alive in the mind of client. What is the main inspirational part?	Documents. Dress rehearsals 2 & 3. Alert reception. Tidy toilets, set up room, agenda, & name plates. Check equipment & cue film clips, etc. Run session to hype up your team (get their adrenalin pumping).	Post all presentation on specially created, password-accessed website, set up for client team. Keep on "presenting" via proactive initiatives you identify in the days following the pitch.

About the author

David Kean is co-founder of The Caffeine Partnership, a consultancy which gives clients a rapid injection of stimulating ideas and solutions to turbo-charge their business growth. He specializes in business development and is an acknowledged authority on the art of pitching, having been ranked as the most valuable new business operator in the UK by *Campaign* magazine. David lectures on business development and pitching in the US, Middle East, Europe and Asia. He is also the co-author of *How to Win Friends and Influence Profits: The art of winning more business from your clients*.